Public Speaking
Strategic Choices
Seventh Edition

Laurie L. Haleta
South Dakota State University

MORTON
PUBLISHING

925 W. Kenyon Avenue, Unit 12
Englewood, CO 80110

www.morton-pub.com

Book Team

Publisher:	Douglas N. Morton
President:	David M. Ferguson
Acquisitions Editor:	Marta R. Martins
Associate Editor—CustomLab:	Adam Jones
Project Manager:	Melanie Stafford
Associate Project Manager:	Rayna Bailey
Production Manager:	Joanne Saliger
Production Assistant:	Will Kelley

Printed in the United States of America

10 9 8 7 6 5 4 3 2 1

ISBN-13: 978-1-61731-177-2

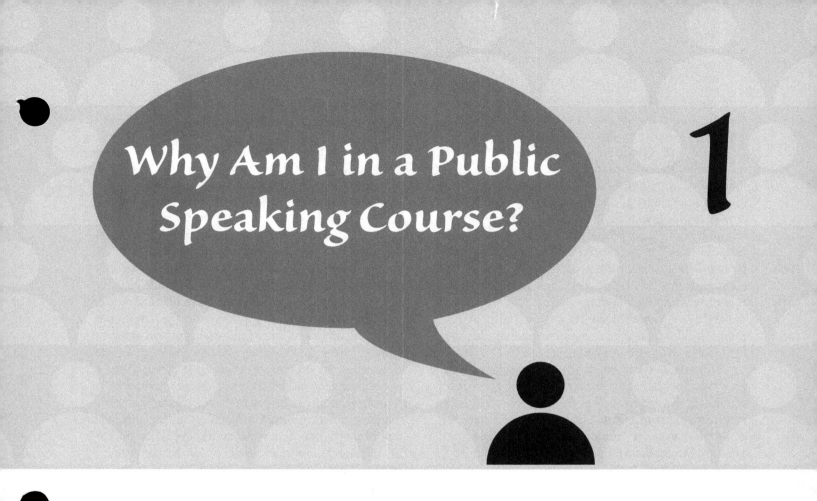

Why Am I in a Public Speaking Course?

1

The most common question we hear from students is, "Why do I have to take a speech class?" Those of us in the communication discipline always smile when we hear students tell us they won't have to give speeches in their major or in their career choices. The fact is, every career, whether in the fields of engineering, pharmacy, agriculture, literature, or others, will require you to speak publicly at some point in time.

For example, I had the opportunity to listen to teams from three different architectural firms make presentations in a bid to be awarded a contract to build a new facility on campus. Each team had the same goal, to persuade the committee to award them the contract. Each team provided the same basic information about what would be included in the facility and how they would go about the building process. Each team included qualified, competent professionals. What differed among the three firms was the way in which they presented their message and how well they crafted their presentation. The contrast was stark. Two firms had dynamic, well-organized, engaging presentations. One firm, unfortunately, did

not, and as a result it was quickly eliminated from the process. After the presentations, the building committee met to decide who would be awarded the contract. The one team's lackluster presentation was a primary discussion point. In the end, a series of poor speeches contributed to one firm losing a contract of over $30 million! Architectural students need to study design, engineering, and a host of other subjects, but in the end, excellent public speaking skills can make a difference. A basic public speaking class will provide you with an opportunity to develop your oral communication skills and prepare you for professional success.

Communication Skills Are Critical in All Disciplines

Excellent communication skills are vital. But don't take my word for it. Employers and businesses are looking for individuals who not only have a strong knowledge base in their respective disciplines but also have outstanding communication skills. According to the National Association of Colleges and Employers (NACE), the ability to effectively communicate with persons inside and outside of an organization is the single most important skill that employers want from new college graduates.

Employers, companies, and businesses are universal in their desire to hire individuals who have excellent communication skills. If you check job advertisements and job postings you will find employers list good communication skills as a requirement in their positions. This is not a new phenomenon. For decades, employers have consistently reported their desire for employees with outstanding communication skills; however, in a shrinking global economy with an extremely competitive job market, the ability to communicate effectively is critical. A public speaking class can help develop confidence for interviewing and applying for jobs.

Employment and financial outcomes are not the only benefits of effective communication. There is something rewarding on a personal level in becoming an effective communicator. Strong communication skills make us more confident in ourselves and our abilities. Strong communication skills enable us to set goals and look for opportunities we might not have imagined. Strong communication skills enable us to have an impact on our own lives and on the lives of others. A basic public speaking class has practical implications for everyday situations. We can learn how to defend personal thoughts and ideas and gain skills in forming relationships. Finally, public speaking classes help prepare students to form and work effectively within groups.

As you embark on your college career, you will find that the skills you develop in public speaking will enhance your ability to give individual and group presentations. You will learn how to effectively debate and create strong arguments. Communication skills will enable you to present research findings and project reports in a clear and organized manner. These skills are necessary for individuals in science and math, engineering and the social sciences, arts and humanities, health professions and education.

In other words, communication plays a central role in everything we do. The only way to improve communication behavior is to practice communication behavior. In short, you need to learn the skills, the processes, and the choices that will improve messages. That is why you are taking a public speaking course!

History and Overview of the Communication Discipline

Another way to appreciate the importance of effective communication skills is to understand the historical perspective of communication arts. The first appearance of public discourse and its role in societies dates to the early fourth century B.C.E. In the Greek city-states and along the Mediterranean, civilizations were moving toward democratic processes. Citizens were coming together to defend themselves and to identify common values and ideals. As a result, male citizens were taught how to effectively present ideas. One area of study was identifying ways to make speeches more appealing and persuasive. During this period Athens, Greece, emerged as a center of culture, education, and citizenship. An expectation of citizenship was active participation in public affairs. Thus, men could be found engaging in oratory in the agora, the precursor to today's public forum. Communication was used as a tool for settling conflict and determining public policy.

Thus, the public speaking course that you are currently enrolled in has its roots in the era of the emergence of Greece. The fourth century also marks the birth of Aristotle in 384 B.C.E. Aristotle's contributions to modern thinking have been well documented in the areas of physics, logic, politics, government, music, theater, and rhetoric. His writings on the subject of rhetoric (the art of discourse) have transcended time, and we are left with his five canons of rhetoric. The canons are traditional elements used in crafting a persuasive speech and include invention (all available means of persuasion, including logos, pathos, and ethos), arrangement, style (or language), delivery, and memory. Public speeches during this period were measured in large part by the structure and effectiveness of arguments.

Through the seventeenth to the twentieth centuries, renewed emphasis was placed on the delivery of speeches. Courses in declamation (delivering an already presented speech) and elocution (the use of posture, movement, gestures, voice, and facial expressions) were the norm during this time. The modern age emerged with an interest in mass communication and media-delivered messages. Radio, television, and the Internet have enabled millions of people to witness public speeches and presentations.

Preface

Students continue to ask an age old question, "Why do I have to take a speech class?" The answer is simple, now more than ever the most desired skill an individual can possess is excellent communication skills. As the world becomes a more competitive place for academic excellence, jobs, success, and individual growth, the single most important talent we can develop is our ability to be an effective communicator. The need for effective communicators transcends all majors, disciplines, professions, and job searches.

Successful public speaking is not simple. It is much more than delivering remarks or sharing ideas. It takes planning, preparation, strategy and practice. The goal of this book is to provide you with the concepts, information, and skills that will result in a successful classroom experience and transform these experiences into all aspects of your life. Whether you believe it or not, you will be expected to speak publicly throughout your life. We want you to be successful and effective in all of these future endeavors.

When you have finished this course, you should have learned

- the fundamental variables in audience analysis and how these affect the selection of topics and the development of speeches;

- the basics of conducting research and information gathering, and how to analyze and evaluate evidence;

- how to organize and structure speeches;

- how to create reasoning strategies based on the evidence and data and how to analyze others' reasoning; and

- the role of language in public speeches and how to improve and analyze language choice in public presentations.

Successful public speaking is not simple or easy. The very nature of communication is complex. You will learn the theoretical and conceptual material that underpins the public speaking discipline. Through class objectives you will be given the tools necessary to construct and present a good speech. You will draw upon your own creative efforts to accomplish this goal.

Chapter 1 is new! In this chapter you will find an answer, or answers, to your questions about the need for a public speaking course. Also included is an overview of the communication discipline as well as areas of study and possible career opportunities. Chapter 2 introduces you to the different levels of communication and includes an expanded section on a common communication problem—communication apprehension. A new section on ethics in public speaking is also included. In Chapter 3 you will be introduced to the basic communication concepts that underlie the entire public speaking process, along with the steps to begin public speaking. These principles are elaborated upon in subsequent chapters.

Listening is a critical communication variable in the public speaking process. Chapter 4 presents the principles of listening, which will serve you well in communication throughout your daily life.

Chapter 5 is devoted to what can be considered the most difficult task students face in public speaking: topic selection and audience analysis. Chapter 6 provides information and guidance on how to organize your ideas, research, and data into a completed speech. The process of conducting and analyzing appropriate research for the public speech is the topic of Chapter 7. Chapter 8 explains the role of evidence and reasoning in public speaking. Chapter 9 addresses the use of language, and Chapter 10 outlines strategies for delivering speeches. Informative and persuasive speaking are the topics of Chapters 11 and 12, respectively. Finally, Chapter 13 covers small-group communication and public presentations.

Appendices A and B are forms for the student to complete a personal inventory and to brainstorm ideas and topics of personal interest. Appendix C presents the assignments and sample outlines that correspond with the Fundamentals of Speech course, as well as new rubrics for evaluating and assessing each presentation. An evaluation form for viewing several great speeches is provided in Appendix D. and Appendix F is a personal information sheet. This latest addition includes updated examples, topics, outlines, and approaches to conducting research.

Completion of this course is a first step and is not a one-time experience. Throughout your university experience and in your future career you will be expected to speak publicly. You will be expected to give presentations, share information, work in teams, and make public speeches. Your ability to develop strong communication skills will enhance your academic, professional, and personal goals. We welcome you to this course and look forward to helping you develop skills that will last a lifetime!

Acknowledgments

After almost 33 years of teaching, I still find a profound sense of joy in working with students. I am particularly devoted to witnessing young students grow and mature through the basic communication course. I simply can't imagine doing anything else.

My gratitude goes to Morton Publishing for their support of this project. Adam, you were terrific to work with.

To my colleagues, I am in awe of your dedication to our students, our department and our university.

My sincere thanks to Lindsay Quenzer, for her outstanding assistance in creating the new, first chapter of this edition.

Joshua, you are the future, and the future has never been in more talented and capable hands.

Alicia, you're right. You were sent here to take care of us and you will never know the solace that brings to me.

To Alex, André, Sasha, and Lindsay, every day is a triumph, woven with love and care. You all mean the world to me.

This edition is dedicated to our mothers: Baba, Dorothy, and Jean.

Contents

Beginning in the twentieth century and continuing to present day, an organized and dramatically rapid growth in the discipline is recorded. The National Communication Association, the discipline's national organization, was formed in 1914. At the turn of the twentieth century, most English departments across the country also taught speech; however, there was very low instruction in this area and it led to conflict. Universities began to push for greater recognition of speech as a distinct academic unit and, consequently, many speech departments were formed. The discipline began to move away from traditional public speaking courses and expanded to include courses that were, and continue to be, influenced by social and intellectual climates. As a result, classes in Interpersonal Communication, Small-Group Communication, and Parliamentary Procedure have emerged.

The speech communication discipline began to integrate contemporary thought into teaching and research. This was accelerated with influences from psychological theory and the work of Sigmund Freud as well as influences from social adjustment theories and the work of John Dewey. Departments began renaming themselves Speech Communication to more accurately reflect the growing breadth of the discipline. Research began to emerge based on the study of personality and its relationship to speech. After World War II, a strong focus emerged that explored psychological concepts relative to communication behaviors. A final trend has emerged since the mid 1990s, with departments going through another renaming process, adopting Communication Studies as a more contemporary label.

Thus, the public speaking course that you are currently enrolled in has its roots in the emergence of Greece as a city-state that promoted the democratic principles we acknowledge today. The discipline of speech, speech communication, and finally communication studies has evolved and grown to embody a broad and compelling area of research and instruction. We're not just about speech anymore, but our core is based on the traditions and belief in effective public speaking.

Branches and Areas of Study

As mentioned earlier, the discipline of communication has grown and encompasses a wide range of study areas. The following is a partial list of the areas of study in the communication field.

Rhetorical and Public Address: This area studies the principles that account for the impact of communication between the speaker and the audience. Studies have examined the historical and social context of platforms, campaigns, and movements. A key function of this area of study is examining the available means of persuasion to present an argument.

Interpersonal Communication: The focus of this area is the verbal and nonverbal cues in communication interactions between two or more people. Research in this area examines how communication behaviors impact personal relationships.

Organizational Communication: The study of organizational communication examines the processes used to analyze communication needs of organizations and social interaction. Areas of research include supervisor/subordinate relationships, culture, climate, and leadership.

Intercultural and Cross-Cultural Communication: The examination of communication among individuals of different cultural backgrounds is the foundation for intercultural communication. Of most interest are the communication similarities and differences across cultures.

Legal and Political Communication: Areas of study include the role of communication in political systems and the role of communication as it relates to the legal system.

Health Communication: This is the fastest growing area of communication. This branch examines the role of communication in the health-care professional/patient relationship and messages directed at health and health-care promotion.

There are limitless possibilities in terms of the kinds of classes students can take in Communication Studies. Take a look at some of the interesting course options available to students:

a. **Family Communication**
   i. A study of theoretical dimensions of intercultural communication as well as specific characteristics of intercultural study.
   ii. Emphasis is placed on complex, mindful, creative, and invitational communication, which welcomes diversity and its richness.

b. **Organizational Communication**
   i. Explores communication processes in organizational contexts, theories of leadership,

decision making and conflict, the application of principles that facilitate communication in organizations, and other selected topics.

c. **Fundamentals of Speech/Public Speaking**
   i. Introduces the study of speech fundamentals and critical thinking through frequent public speaking practice, including setting, purpose, audience, and subject.
   ii. Sharpens students' skills in platform speaking events, covering the preparation for and delivery of competitive speaking formats, including oral interpretation, persuasive, expository, impromptu, extemporaneous, and after-dinner speaking.

d. **Argumentation and Debate**
   i. Explores argument as a communication activity, construction of sound arguments in a variety of venues, and analyzing the contribution of argument to public dialogue on contemporary issues.

e. **Interpersonal Communication**
   i. Studies modes of interpersonal communication through readings, and experiential discussions of the role of interpersonal communications in common situations within society.

f. **Rhetorical Criticism**
   i. Evaluates American speakers from colonial to contemporary times.

g. **Communication Research**
   i. An exploration of basic theoretical and practical principles of quantitative and qualitative research methods in the study of communication.
   ii. Students learn to form research questions; work with resources such as academic journals, popular culture, and the Internet; use recognized research formats, and write research proposals.

h. **Communication and Gender**
   i. A study of gender theories as well as gendered communication practices within the contexts of interpersonal and organizational relationships and social and cultural forces.

j. **Communication in Interviewing**
   i. Provides an in-depth study of the interviewing process, including information gathering, persuasion, appraisal, and employment interviews.

ii. Emphasizes theoretical knowledge from the perspectives of the interviewer and interviewee, as well as skill development in interviewing techniques.

k. **Oral Interpretation of Literature**
   i. Examines the theory and practice of the performance of texts, the artistic, aesthetic, and carefully considered sharing of our personal understanding of literary selection, involving analysis, planning, rehearsing, and effective sharing of meaning with an audience.

l. **Small-Group Communication**
   i. Explores prominent concepts and theories of human small-group interaction, cultivating critical assessments of communication strategies in task, social, and therapeutic groups.

m. **Theories of Communication**
   i. Examines communication theories and philosophies, emphasizing clarification through theory of daily communication processes and relating theory to traditional and developing research methods.

n. **Political Communication**
   i. Studies the rhetoric of selected political figures, movements, and campaigns that have changed lives and cultures.
   ii. Students develop an understanding of rhetorical strategies and their cultural impact within public life.

o. **Intercultural Communication**
   i. A study of theoretical dimensions of intercultural communication as well as specific characteristics of intercultural study.
   ii. Emphasis is placed on complex, mindful, creative, and invitational communication, which welcomes diversity and its richness.

p. **Speech and Debate Activities**
   i. Initiates active participation in competitive public speaking, including debate, oral interpretation, and noncompetitive public performances.

q. **Health Communication**
   i. This area examines the contexts and processes of communication about health, focusing on how professionals, patients, and practitioners interact in ways that constitute and influence health and medicine.

Considering a Communication Studies Major or Minor

Now that you have an idea of the types of courses available in the communication field and the advantages of developing communication skills, let me address a question that I hear from students: Why should I become a communication studies major or minor?

First and foremost, there are unlimited career options and possibilities. Second, this is a sought-after degree by employers! Consider an article posted online by YAHOO! Education titled, "College Degrees That Are Sexy to Employers." After examining recent hiring trends, the article listed degrees that will get you noticed by employers, and a communications major was listed as the number two degree! As noted earlier, employers desire individuals with strong communication skills and the ability to persuade and inform effectively.

The following is a list of the many opportunities that await a communication studies major and represent a partial list of the many careers that people with communication majors have entered:

Teaching
   High School Speech and Theater
   College Instructor
   College Professor
Human Resources
   Manager/Director
   Headhunter
   Interviewer
   Job Placement
   Staff Training & Development
Nonprofit Organizations
   Director
   Community Relations Director
   Communication Affairs Liaison
   Director of Communication & Outreach
   Fund-raising Director
   Event Planner/Coordinator
University/College Student Affairs
   Diversity Director
   Admissions Counselor
   Greek Life Advisor
   Academic Advisor
   Student Activities Director
   Residential Housing Director
   Alumni Coordinator
Other/Independent
   Sales & Marketing/Advertising
   Wedding Consultant

Human Rights Officer
Arbitration & Mediation
Life Coach
Camp Director
Speechwriter
Political Campaign Coordinator
Motivational Speaker
Communication Consultant

As you can see, the possibilities are endless. Communication majors are positioned to enter the workforce in many different areas. In addition, a communication major or minor enhances other majors or preprofessional programs, including, but not limited to:

Pre-Law
Pharmacy
Pre-Med
Psychology & Sociology
Teaching
Business & Economics
Counseling
Ministry/Missions work

As you can see, a communication major or minor will enhance any other major. Given what we know about employers desire to hire individuals with strong communication skills, it only makes sense for students to consider how they can make themselves more marketable in the workforce.

What Communication Majors Say?

Students, past and present, can best articulate what a degree in communication means to them. These conversations are always some of the most rewarding and inspiring discussions teachers and professors may have with students. They are worth sharing with others. We recently asked our current majors why they chose a communication major. These are a few of their comments:

👤 "My interests were not specific enough to make a decision, and Communication Studies gives me the option to work anywhere."

👤 "Because of its flexibility with choosing classes and what I can [do] with it when I am done. It also goes with any minor that you want to add to it."

👤 "I didn't know what I wanted to do, but I had to pick something. Communication Studies gave me a broad list of options and it turned out to be perfect for me."

"I realized that I not only really enjoyed speaking, but I was good at it. So I looked into the program and after seeing all the aspects of communication, I was very intrigued. I love learning how people communicate, behave, and interact; and the information is so practical and useful."

Here's what some of our graduates say:

"I'm so glad I decided to major in Communication Studies. My degree prepared me to have options and I found a great job in business."

"Because I graduated with a degree in communication, I was hired in a management position. I was able to move into middle management almost immediately."

"I asked my employer one day why I was chosen for my job in a health organization. I knew the applicant pool was very large and so I wondered why I was chosen. She told me that my communication background gave me the skills they were looking for."

"My communication degree has enabled me to be flexible in selecting a career. I found a great position, working for one of the largest companies in the country."

"The professors I had in my communication major inspired me, and I decided to work on a graduate degree. I completed my Ph.D., and now I teach. I never thought of myself as a college professor when I was a freshman or sophomore, but this discipline opened doors for me."

As you can see, there are a number of reasons students choose a major in Communication Studies. There are also wonderful stories about the successes communication majors have as they pursue career options. All of these opportunities are available to you!

In closing, we welcome you to the public speaking course. A door is opening for you to explore and discover the world of communication. We guarantee you will be pleased and surprised at the talent and skill you possess.

Review Items: Chapter 1

Name _____ Date _____

1. What is your current college major?

2. What is your career objective after graduation?

3. Specifically, what job or kinds of jobs would interest you?

4. What kinds of communication activities will be required of you in your future job (public speaking, small-group or committee work, working with the public, etc.)?

5. Review the list of courses available in the communication discipline. Identify which courses would be beneficial as you plan for your future career.

6. Given your career goals, list the ways in which a communication minor or perhaps a major in communication can help you to achieve success.

The Communication Process

2

As discussed in Chapter One, modern public speaking practices stem from the ancient Greeks and are based on rhetorical traditions. Many of these traditional elements have been retained, providing a foundation for a process that has evolved based on contemporary needs and technological advances. Public speaking is just one of many contexts of communication interwoven with other contexts. It is important to understand all of the contexts of communication to appreciate and understand the public speaking context.

Contexts of Communication

The four basic contexts of communication are intrapersonal, interpersonal, public speaking, and mass media.

Intrapersonal Communication

Intrapersonal communication is when we communicate within ourselves. We convince ourselves that we need to get in shape and start a running program. We tell ourselves we need to stay in over the weekend and study for an upcoming exam. We listen to the latest news and information programs, internalizing

the information and making a decision about who to vote for in the next election. We formulate arguments internally to be used when we want to ask for something. Through intrapersonal communication, we develop and form beliefs and attitudes that shape our lives. Through intrapersonal communication, we make decisions about how we live and what we think of the world around us.

Interpersonal Communication

We also communicate on an **interpersonal** level. Generally, when we communicate on an interpersonal level we are in a one-on-one situation with another person or with just a few people. This communication context is more complex because we must communicate to another person thoughts and ideas that we have internalized. Most interpersonal communication takes place with an individual who is close to us—a friend, a family member, or someone we know well.

Interpersonal communication is difficult for many people, except at the most superficial level. We are comfortable talking with others about minor things but may not wish to discuss personal problems. In order for interpersonal communication to be successful, we need to be able to listen carefully to the other person or people in the conversation and modify or temper our remarks to the feedback we are receiving from others. It is easy to see how the interpersonal context interacts with intrapersonal communication. Interpersonal communication becomes input for intrapersonal communication. This, in turn, alters the intrapersonal system and influences other contexts.

Public Speaking

Public speaking is not an isolated context of communication. It builds upon the foundation of intrapersonal communication. Public speaking can best be thought of as an individual conveying prepared remarks to an audience using some kind of formal structure. To prepare a speech, the public speaker must act or think intrapersonally. Because the audience is a vital consideration when planning speech strategies, interpersonal interaction is necessary in effective public speaking. Gauging nonverbal feedback from audience members and judging their reaction to a message is vitally important in adjusting public messages. The public speaking context, perhaps more than any other, relies heavily on the other contexts for support.

Mass Media

Mass media have been expanding rapidly, and we now are bombarded with messages from a variety of sources. Satellite radio provides us with an expanded repertoire of news and opinions. Television is a fixture in college residences and homes. The Internet has changed how we communicate and acquire information. We find more and more news outlets posting their periodicals online, and multiple databases of information are also available online. We can post videos on YouTube. Social media, including Facebook and Twitter, have changed how we communicate with each other and interact with the world. We are able to Skype conversations and presentations. In a relatively short period of time, mass media have had a significant effect on how we gather information and prepare ourselves for public speaking.

You will be using mass media sources in your preparation for public speaking. Because the media are ever present in our lives, they generate a rich source of topics. Like the other contexts just introduced, the mass media are integral to public speaking.

Public speaking does not occur in a vacuum. As a beginning speaker, you will learn to use the various contexts to your benefit. Many things happen during

a public speech, and these variables are present in other contexts as well.

Variables in the Communication Process

Speech is not an isolated, singular event. It is part of a continuous process that, in the case of public speaking, begins with an idea that is developed, manipulated, researched, prepared, and practiced before being presented to an audience. To make the analysis discrete, however, we are treating speech as an isolated event here. We begin by describing the elements of speech.

Elements of Speech

The basic elements of speech are the source, the message, the channel, and the receiver.

1. The SOURCE. The speaker initiates a message for consumption by an audience. Although the goal of speech is determined long before the speaker stands up to address the audience, we concentrate here on what the source does in the speaking process. As the source, you have the task of formulating a message for an audience.

2. The MESSAGE. The message is verbal (presented orally) and also has a nonverbal component. This book emphasizes the verbal components of a message, along with strategies for its preparation and delivery. The message is shaped by many things, including the assignment and the audience. The major task is to prepare a message that is suitable for the assignment and the audience. As the source of the message, the speaker is responsible for **encoding** (the process of conveying) the message. The audience engages in **decoding** (the process of interpreting) the message.

3. The CHANNEL. The message is communicated through a medium called the channel—in the case of public speaking, airwaves. The message is both heard and seen. Many beginning speakers have little control over the channel. As you will discover, however, interference (noise) in the channel is a concern for speakers. There is also a nonverbal component to the channel, based on the speaker's physical behavior during a speech. In some instances, visual aids, such as PowerPoint slides, contribute to the channel.

4. The RECEIVER. At the other end of the public speech is the person who attributes meaning to

the message. What the speaker says gains importance according to what happens with individual audience members. Although we tend to consider public speeches as being for consumption by many people—the audience—the primary consideration is the individual audience member. This person is called a receiver, and the audience is a collection of receivers. A good public speaker tries to develop a message that is applicable to the entire audience, but must keep in mind that each receiver interprets the message in his or her own way.

Public speaking formerly was explained as involving only these four elements: A source sends a message through a channel to the receivers, and the public speaking event is complete. This event is linear in nature and can be represented graphically, as seen in **Figure 2.1**. This view of public speaking is far too simple, though. Speakers don't just utter words to an audience and that is the end of it. A more complete view of public speaking incorporates at least two additional variables, which makes public speaking part of an ongoing circular process. These variables are feedback and noise.

5. FEEDBACK. When a receiver reacts to a message, even in a crowded classroom or an assembly hall, he or she in essence becomes another source, who develops another message and sends it through a channel to the original source, who now has become a receiver. This is known as feedback. In public speaking, feedback is often nonverbal because few audience members are likely to interrupt a speaker verbally. In feedback, the parties to a public speaking exchange have dual roles—both source and receiver—and exchange roles in the encoding and decoding process. If the original source of the message alters his or her message to accommodate the feedback, a new source/message/channel/receiver relationship is born. **Figure 2.2** illustrates how public speaking becomes circular.

6. NOISE. The public speaking exchange usually is bombarded with interference, termed *noise*. Simply defined, noise is anything that disturbs effective communication and can be divided into two types—mechanical and semantic. **Mechanical noise** is what we normally consider "real" noise, examples include shuffling papers, coughing, and heating or air-conditioning disturbances. This type of noise interferes with the channel of communication. **Semantic noise** refers to the words chosen for the message. Examples are **jargon** or **slang**, as well as technical terms that may be unfamiliar to some audience members. Noise adds

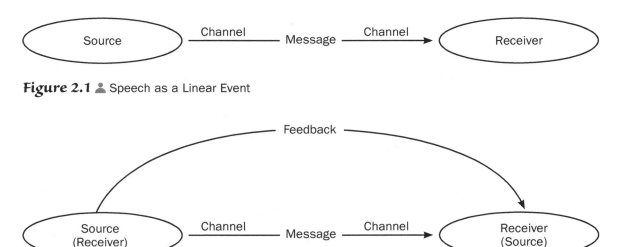

Figure 2.1 👤 Speech as a Linear Event

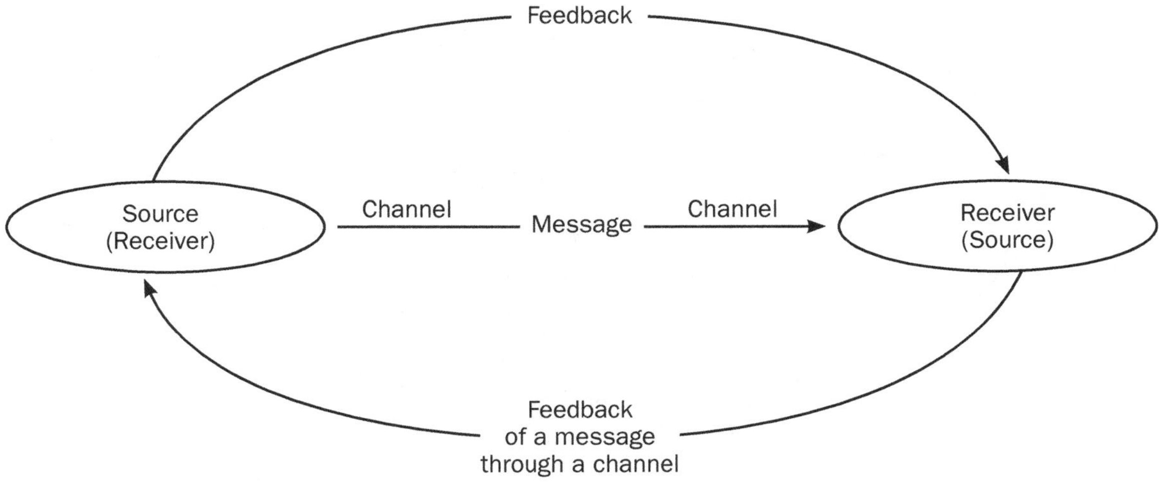

Figure 2.2 👤 The Circular Nature of Public Speaking

another dimension to the process model of communication. Interestingly, noise can also be internal and either physiological or psychological in nature. Physiological noise becomes a factor if you are extremely apprehensive or fearful during a presentation, or if you are ill. Your message may be impacted by this internal noise. Similarly, audience members who are distracted from your message by their own internal thoughts are dealing with psychological noise. As students, you may experience this quite often in classes. Instead of focusing on a biology lecture, for example, you may be thinking about an upcoming exam in another class or anticipating an evening out.

A Model of Public Speaking

Figure 2.3 presents a model of public speaking illustrating the basic variables and assuming others. For example, we assume that each source chooses a topic based on interest and other considerations. We assume that each receiver has some preconception about the topic before a speech begins. We assume that the message is relayed in a spoken language common to audience members. Even the most complex models cannot (and are not intended to) show everything that transpires during a public speech. Communication is a complex process that is labeled as transactual. Transactual processes are those in which messages are being sent and received simultaneously. These messages are intentional, and this transfer of information takes place within a defined situation. Trying to develop a model that shows all the variables is not modeling; it is constructing. Here we concentrate on the basic elements in the process. Knowing about the variables in public speaking will help you understand what you are trying to accomplish in a speech.

Public Speaking in Society

At some point during your day you will be confronted with elements of public speaking. Political leaders will make televised addresses. You will hear lectures in classes. If you watch television, you will see countless advertisements. Whenever people talk to people, it is called public speaking. This text does not limit the analysis of public speaking to standing in front of a live audience and giving a speech. Public speaking occurs in every medium imaginable.

If you try to convince your friends to go out for supper with you, even though this situation is classified as interpersonal, you are using the same principles that are used in public speaking. When advertisers try to convince you to buy a new car, public speaking principles are at work. This text will expose you to these strategies of public speaking in addition to speaking before an audience.

Ethics and Public Speaking

Notwithstanding the assertion that the principles of public speaking are amoral (without morals) public speaking also carries an ethical imperative. Speeches

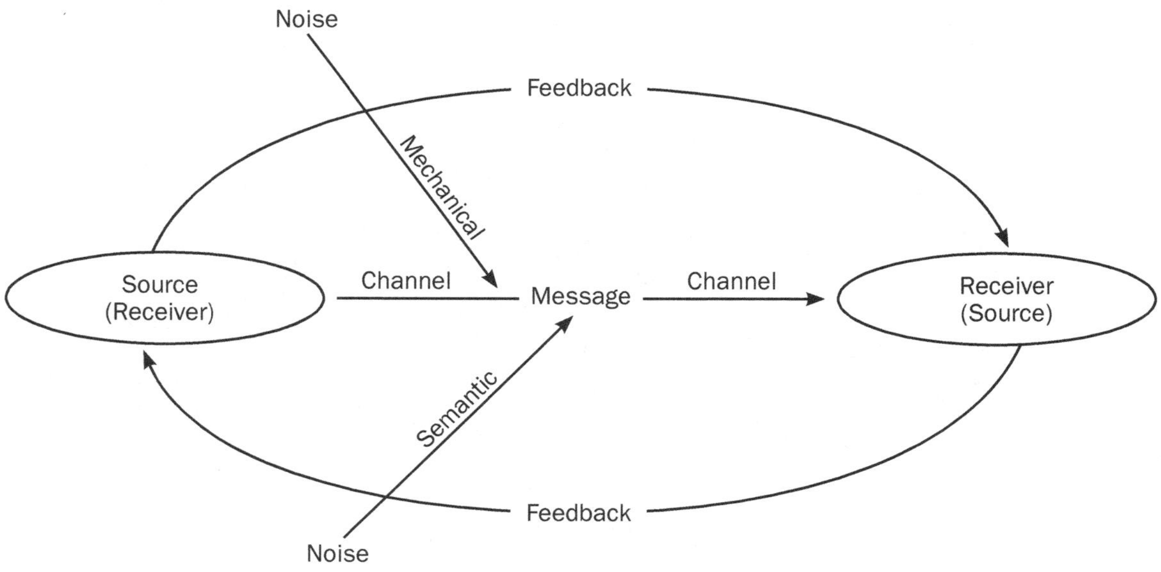

Figure 2.3 Model of Public Speaking

themselves are not good or bad, but a speaker can abuse the strategies available and persuade people to do wrong, or the speaker can disseminate information correctly and accurately. Ethical considerations in public speaking take many forms, including, but not limited to, plagiarism of information (not giving proper credit for non-original information), the use of reliable and accurate evidence and reasoning patterns, truthfulness, goals and intentions for the speech, sensitivity to differences and respecting cultural diversity, and valuing freedom of speech. Given the enormous responsibility that speakers carry, it is worth looking at these criteria more closely.

Plagiarism

Simply put, plagiarism is stealing! Plagiarism can take many forms and it can be either intentional or unintentional. Regardless of the intent or the manner, it is wrong and can have profound implications for speakers. Plagiarism occurs when speakers literally copy entire speeches or texts and use them as their own. Plagiarism also occurs when speakers fail to properly document or give credit for non-original information, including direct quotations, paraphrased ideas or opinions, and statistics. Plagiarism occurs when you fail to do your own work independently. You cannot "work together" with a friend or roommate on a speech. We have seen countless occasions of students working together on a speech and then independently giving the identical speech in different sections of their speech class. The consequences of plagiarism are profound. It can result in a failing grade on an assignment or in a course. Plagiarism can lead to university sanctions and even expulsion. In the real world, plagiarism can have dramatic effects, including being fired from a job and the destruction of a career.

Reliable and Accurate Evidence and Reasoning

Speakers are obligated to use accurate and truthful evidence. Facts and the truth matter in public speaking. For example, during an April 2012 town hall meeting, U.S. Congressman Allen West (R-FL) was asked a question about his fellow congress members and their leanings as Marxists or Socialists. Congressman West remarked that he believed there are "about 78 to 81 members of the Democratic Party that are members of the Communist Party." The congressman made this comment without any evidence or proof to support his statement. Clearly,

this statement was made to enflame and manipulates people's feelings and beliefs. Public speakers have incredible power and opportunity to change the course of people's lives. We are obligated to use accurate and truthful information and to carefully reason from that evidence.

Truthfulness

Public speakers have a responsibility to be honest. Not only does this include using factual evidence, but it also literally means speaking the truth. As speakers, we are ethically required to be honest and to avoid the fabrication of information or evidence, misrepresentation of facts, or the omission of facts and information.

Goals and Intentions

Audiences deserve to know what our intended outcome is when we ask for their attention and time. One of the goals of a good speech is to clearly signal to the audience the intent of the presentation. Most public speeches are crafted in a way to either inform or persuade the audience. Audiences should know this. More importantly, there should be no hidden agenda on the part of the speaker. It is unethical for a speaker to use public speeches to manipulate, intimidate, or coerce audiences. History is full of individuals who have used the public forum for unethical purposes, most notably Adolph Hitler, who moved an entire world to war through messages of hatred and intolerance.

Diversity

An ethical public speaker will acknowledge and be respectful of the diverse values, beliefs, attitudes, and backgrounds of an audience. It is imperative that the public space is used for the purposes of understanding, tolerance, and inclusion. A speaker can create a climate of respect by acknowledging diverse opinions. It is also vital to carefully craft messages that are free from offensive language, stereotypes, and judgmental statements.

Freedom of Speech

American citizens enjoy a right that is the envy of world. The First Amendment to the U.S. Constitution (1791) guarantees that "Congress shall make no law...abridging the freedom of speech, or the press." In essence, we are guaranteed the right to speak our mind without consequence. This right is extended to ethical and unethical speakers alike. As public speakers we are obligated to protect the rights of all people, whether we agree with their messages or not.

The ethical criteria you apply to yourself and your speaking are personal. Just as fair play is expected of the speaker in society, so it is of you.

Communication Apprehension

One of the most important concerns regarding public speaking centers on fear! You may have heard the commonplace joke that the thing most feared by Americans, above and beyond death and taxes, is giving a speech. Unfortunately, it is not a joke. Most people groan when they find out they need to give a speech or make a presentation. Many people will go out of their way to avoid giving speeches. So, if your reaction to being in a basic speech course is concern, you are not alone. You are probably dealing with a certain degree of communication apprehension. The concept of **communication apprehension**, first identified by James C. McCroskey, is defined as "an individual's level of fear or anxiety associated with either real or anticipated communication with another person or persons."[1] Communication apprehension (CA) is not restricted to the public speaker or the student enrolled in a speech class. It is a normal, widespread phenomenon that affects nearly everyone to a greater or lesser extent. Over the years, in many polls and surveys conducted to identify people's fears, the fear of public speaking consistently appears at the top of the list.

Anyone who has participated in sports, music, entertainment, or presentations for groups or organizations will be able to identify with this phenomenon. Communication apprehension is a form of performance anxiety. Athletes experience excitement and an adrenalin rush before a game or match. Musicians deal with a variety of emotions before a concert or recital. Actors experience anxiety and excitement before the curtain goes up. This feeling is not limited to the young, the amateur, or the student. Most professionals face the same anxieties associated with public performance. Popular singers, entertainers, athletes, and speakers have documented their apprehension.

As a university student, you have faculty and instructors in every class. Even these "professional lecturers" likely are faced with communication

apprehension before entering the classroom and beginning the day's activities.

The symptoms of CA are easy to recognize and certainly are familiar. They manifest themselves in the form of shaking hands, sweaty palms, a dry mouth and difficulty swallowing, a red rash or flushed face, rapid or increased breathing, and that feeling known as "butterflies in the stomach." These are examples of physiological reactions that occur when our bodies and minds are preparing to respond to a situation—in this case, a public speaking environment—that will require more than the usual amount of effort and concentration. Keep in mind that these responses are normal, and as a student in a public speaking course, recognize these symptoms for what they are.

To simply understand that these reactions are normal is not enough. We have to learn how to cope with the symptoms and then to use them as a positive factor in public speaking. In short, when it is recognized and dealt with, communication apprehension can be turned into a positive force in a public speaking presentation.

Resources for Communication Apprehension

Talk to someone who can help with your apprehension. If you are feeling that your apprehension and nervousness is beyond what is considered normal, or if you feel that you are in a "flight" mode, contact your instructor. Your speech instructor is trained to recognize and assist you with communication apprehension. If your apprehension is extreme, your instructor can make referrals to further assist you in dealing with this very common phenomenon. By sharing your concerns, you will find that help is available and public speaking can actually be an activity that provides you with great dividends.

Channeling Communication Apprehension

Students frequently remark that they wish they could eliminate their nervousness when preparing for a speech. Again, to be apprehensive is normal, but it can be channeled. The anxiety when preparing for public speaking reflects some important messages.

---

1 In "Measures of Communication-Bound Anxiety," *Speech Monographs*, 37 (1970), 269–277.

1. This message is something that is important or significant to you. Speakers who feel little or no nervousness may not view the upcoming speech as important, or perhaps they are not allowing their nervousness to surface and are keeping it hidden inside. It is better to let the anxiety surface and recognize that the outcome of the speaking experience is important. This apprehension can be focused, helping you concentrate fully and providing the extra energy for this intense concentration. By the time you finish delivering a speech, you may feel exhausted. Then you can be sure that your body provided the extra adrenalin and energy to concentrate fully and perform at your best.

2. You may look around the classroom and feel isolated. Perhaps you are thinking that you are the only one who feels nervous and even a little scared. You should reassure yourself that you are not the only one who is feeling apprehensive about public speaking. You may be concerned about the topic you have chosen, or perhaps you are worried about what your peers will think of you. Or you may be concerned about the grade you will receive on the speech or what your instructor will think about your speech. Maybe you are afraid that you will make a fool of yourself. Most of us have these feelings. You need to acknowledge this fear and make it work for you.

Preparation and Practice

During the course of the semester you will hear the word *rehearse* many times. This is probably the best advice a student of communication can receive. The best strategies for controlling communication apprehension are thorough preparation, research, and practice. If you have followed every step of the assignment carefully—preparing an appropriate speech, supporting it with solid research, and practicing the delivery of the ideas you have developed so carefully—you can feel confident and self-assured that you have done your best. You know what you are doing and why you are doing it. If you begin to feel apprehensive prior to delivering your speech, you will know that it is not because you lack preparation.

Focus on the Message

When you stand up to give your speech, you have one task: to deliver the message to your audience.

This may be easier said than done. But if you can focus on delivering the messages or thoughts rather than allowing yourself to think about how nervous you are, what the audience thinks of you, or how you will remember the next point, you will deliver your speech with confidence. When you channel your energy into delivering your ideas, the nervousness will fade, your audience will respond positively, and you will be able to relate well to your audience.

Gentle Self-Evaluation

When evaluating how well we complete a task, we sometimes are our own worst enemies. This holds true for public speaking. We tend to believe that everyone knows how nervous we are, that we have made a number of terrible mistakes, or that everyone dislikes our topic. Speakers are genuinely surprised to find that their audience had no idea that the speaker was nervous, made mistakes, or was afraid while presenting the speech. Recognize that your nervousness is normal. In fact, after years of teaching the basic speech course, I am worried when a student approaches me and tells me he or she is not nervous. Given the research, a lack of nervousness is not a typical reaction! If our audience enjoys the messages we prepare and deliver, we should be able to enjoy the preparation and delivery as well.

The Student Speaker as Citizen/Analyst

Productive citizens are capable of, and often interested in, analyzing society. For that reason, this course is not taught from a simple "stand up and give a speech" point of view. We expect you to be able to analyze the volumes of material aimed at you as consumers and citizens. As an analyst trained in public speaking, you will be better prepared to make decisions—about candidates for public office, financial investments, and purchases, for example. People trying to get your attention often are also trying to persuade you to do something. If you can recognize and analyze the strategies they are using, you should be able to make better decisions. Learning to speak also means learning to analyze.

Summary

The four basic contexts of communication are: intrapersonal, interpersonal, public speaking, and mass media. All communication has several elements in common, including the source, the message, the channel, and the receiver, as well as feedback and mechanical and semantic noise.

Public speakers have an obligation to be ethical in their presentations. Elements of ethical behavior include avoidance of plagiarism, use of evidence and reasoning, truthfulness, clearly articulated goals, respecting differences, and freedom of speech.

Many speakers can identify with the discomfort of communication apprehension. This can be channeled positively by preparing thoroughly and practicing, focusing on the message, and assessing yourself honestly. Learning the fundamentals of public speaking will aid you in all aspects of your life.

Review Items: Chapter 2

Name _____ Date _____

1. Identify and explain the four contexts of communication.

    1. _____

    _____

    _____

    2. _____

    _____

    _____

    3. _____

    _____

    _____

    4. _____

    _____

    _____

2. Diagram the communication process, using the six variables explained in this chapter.

3. To the diagram, add variables that you think might enhance your understanding of the communication process.

4. Discuss the role of ethics in public speaking. What strategies can you use to ensure that you are making ethical choices in your speeches?

5. Describe your own communication apprehension. What are you most apprehensive about? Have you ever experienced communication apprehension in a public speaking context?

6. Suggest ways in which you might overcome communication apprehension.

7. Explain how you have participated as a citizen/analyst.

The First Speech: Basic Strategies

3

In preparation for the first speech, this chapter presents strategies leading to its delivery. Although these are presented sequentially here, keep in mind that public speaking is not a step-by-step process to follow. Public speaking is a complex and transactional process that involves interaction between and among the following strategies.

Knowing About the Audience

"Getting through" to an audience requires that the speaker know something about the composition of the group. Audience analysis is a critical first step in speech preparation, allowing you the opportunity to gain an understanding of your audience and then making choices to meet the needs and expectations of the audience. Some basic audience variables are:

- age composition of the group
- number of people in the group
- gender composition of the group (male/female? mixed? proportion?)
- educational level of the group
- occupations represented in the group
- geographic area represented by the group
- economic status of the group
  - cultural diversity and ethnic backgrounds of the group
  - political affiliations of the group
  - religious affiliations of the group
  - sexual orientation or identities represented in the group
- special interests of the group

Some of these variables are not applicable to classroom speaking situations. And, as an additional aid, the instructor might have class members give introductory comments about themselves or their peers, or present a first speech about personal feelings or beliefs. This provides an opportunity for you to analyze your audience and get a feeling for their attitudes, beliefs, and values. Understanding the attitudes of your audience will help you know what they like or dislike. For example, are you for or against a ban on texting and driving? Your answer to this question represents your attitude about texting and driving. Beliefs represent what we hold to be true. Do you believe carbon emissions negatively affect our climate? If so, you hold a belief about carbon emissions. Values represent what we believe to be right or wrong. If you believe that it is your responsibility to vote in elections, then you value the democratic process. In speeches outside the classroom, a more thorough analysis of these variables increases the likelihood of effective communication.

Audience analysis is critical, because every audience is different. Considering the unique makeup of an audience allows you to construct a message that is listener oriented. As a result, you can choose and adapt your topic to make it important, relevant, and interesting for your audience. Careful audience analysis allows a speaker to make language choices that effectively communicate the message, relate information directly to the listeners, and decrease the likelihood of alienating audience members.

The audience also must trust the information and its sources. In Chapter 7 we will examine the sources of information used to gather support for the speech. For your first speech, however, you must consider what types and sources of information a given audience considers valid. One person may watch cable news networks, generally, and MSNBC, specifically. Another may trust newspapers such as the *New York Times* and *Wall Street Journal*. Still others get their news from Internet sources and websites. Less difficult are judgments about specialized sources of information—sources linked most directly to a specific audience. For example, motor sports, health and exercise, and genealogy enthusiasts each have their specialized publications. For audiences such as these, you can reasonably assume that those sources of information are trustworthy.

Further, the speaker should try to understand audience expectations. In the classroom situation the audience expects a certain type of speech in keeping with the assignment. Failing to meet these expectations may result in the student audience feeling let down. More potentially problematic is the speech outside the classroom, where failing to comprehend audience expectations may have more serious repercussions.

In any case, speakers have to recognize the composition of the audience and choose and plan strategies that allow their messages to effectively reach that audience. Speech can be viewed as a consumer product, and the speaker should strive to present the most "consumable" product.

Focusing on the Topic

Selecting a topic comes easily to some speakers. To others, it is the most difficult part of the speech preparation process. The audience and the assignment may

dictate this choice in part. Additional considerations include:

1. The topic must be of interest to the speaker. If your topic bores you, that boredom will be obvious to the audience. This is a critical element. If you are excited and passionate about your topic, that energy will transfer to your audience. Additionally, if you are excited about your topic, you will feel more confident in the preparation and delivery of the speech.

2. Sufficient material must be available to support development of the topic. Support can be categorized as (a) original, or personal, and (b) non-original, or support from other information sources. Some speeches require only personal support, and the speaker can rely on his or her own attitudes, beliefs, values, and experiences. Other speeches depend heavily on outside material gathered through the research process. The support aspect of preparation for public speaking will be dealt with in detail later.

Writing the Thesis Sentence

The next step is to narrow the broad topic of a speech. This is done by developing a **thesis sentence**. For our purposes, the thesis sentence can be defined as a simple declarative statement that encompasses the content of the speech.

For example, you may wish to talk generally about identity theft. This topic is broad, but it might be narrowed to: "Identity theft creates serious problems." This thesis then becomes the focused aspect of the topic and directs further development of the idea.

Selecting an Appropriate Organizational Strategy

The thesis sentence does not automatically dictate the organizational development of the body of the speech. We will briefly examine four of the most basic organizational patterns that may be used to develop the body of the speech. Each pattern has applications to various speaking situations, and each helps focus the development of the thesis.

1. CHRONOLOGICAL PATTERN. The main points of the body of the speech are developed in a time sequence. A speaker addressing the concept of gun control may choose to discuss the history

of gun control legislation in the United States by examining laws starting with the first legislation passed, followed by the second legislation passed, and so on.

2. **SPATIAL PATTERN.** The speech is organized according to location in space, or geography. An example is the description of the university library given by your speech instructor in which the library holdings are discussed by floor— textbooks on the upper level, current periodicals on the middle level, and bound periodicals on the lower level. Thus, the three-floor library is described spatially from top to bottom.

3. **TOPICAL PATTERN.** The same library also could be described topically—say, by discussing periodical holdings, reference holdings, and government documents. This could be done without reference to actual location. The focus here is the subject matter, not the location of specific holdings. Topically, you might discuss the problems created by identity theft by listing the areas of harm, such as illegal purchases, damage to credit history, and costs to businesses.

4. **LOGICAL PATTERN.** The speech is organized in a problem/solution sequence. In this pattern— used primarily for persuasive speaking situations—you would introduce the problem and then offer a solution to the problem. Specific types of persuasive speaking will be explored in more depth later in the text.

The organizational pattern you select should offer you the best method of developing the body of the speech both in outline form on paper and orally.

Preparing an Outline

The **outline** is the "skeleton" of the oral speech. We will use the thesis sentence about identity theft to illustrate development of the main points of a speech.

Identity theft creates serious problems.

From this thesis, three main points can be developed:

I. Identity theft can be used for criminal activities.

II. Identity theft can be used for financial fraud.

III. Identity theft can be used for identity cloning and concealment.

Each of these main points directly supports or provides proof for the thesis. Each is a subdivision of the thesis. Each makes sense even without further development of the main point.

Obviously, though, further development of the main points is necessary to the speech. Each main point should have at least two subpoints that support only the main point of which they are a subordinate element. Using the first main point, we can demonstrate this support structure.

I. Identity theft can be used for criminal activities.

    A. Illegal immigration is facilitated through identity theft.

    B. Terrorists use identity theft as a way to conceal their activities.

    C. Medical care and drugs are obtained illegally through identity theft.

We can see that the subpoints directly support only this main point. The other two main points deal with different aspects relevant to identity theft.

The structure developed for proving a thesis sentence is necessary because it gives strong and strict direction to the speech. We will discuss structure and outlining later, but this preliminary material should allow you to get started on the early speeches.

Choosing Forms of Support for the Speech

Ideally, the types of support you choose are determined after completing the outline and overall structure. You might have a vague idea of what you will use to support the subpoints, and now is the time to finalize your supporting materials.

Again, support can come from two sources: (a) personal experience and observation, and (b) non-original sources. Support that comes from non-original sources is called **evidence**. The three most basic forms of evidence are examples, statistics, and testimony.

1. **EXAMPLES:** Single occurrences of an event. The event serves as a graphic depiction of the point you are trying to make. An example might stem from something you have observed personally. In the speech we are developing here, a non-original example may be used to show the problems with identity theft. You could support the main point about financial fraud, for example,

by pointing to an instance in which a family member had his credit card information stolen and found that thousands of dollars of charges appeared on the bill.

2. STATISTICS: Numerical support for a speech. In the identity theft speech you may point to statistics stating that 10 million people are victims of identity theft each year. Statistics tend to highlight the significance of something.

3. TESTIMONY: The opinion of an expert. Any of us can give an opinion, but most of us are experts in only limited cases. Your best friend may be a talented athlete but without proper qualifications, he or she may not be a good source of testimony about identity theft. Instead, you might turn to the U.S. Federal Trade Commission, the Department of Justice, or the Social Security Administration for evidence from a qualified, or expert, source.

Using Support in the Speech

After choosing the forms of support for your speech, you should be prepared to let the audience know where you obtained the information. This **documentation** gives credit where credit is due. It allows audience members to make their own judgments about your evidence.

As an example of oral documentation:

> According to the January 9, 2013, issue of *USA Today* online, "The IRS has failed to provide swift and effective assistance to victims of identity theft even as the number of crimes continues to soar, according to a federal report issued Wednesday." (No author was available)

The documentation demonstrates the source and location of the information, which gives the speech credibility. We encourage you to tell the audience the particulars about personal observations and experiences as well.

In your early speeches, the choice of forms of support is an individual matter. Your own intuition might be enough to select information that will support each element of the substructure. As speeches become more complex, the requirements and strategies will differ. We will discuss evidence in more detail later.

Planning the Introduction and the Conclusion

By this point you probably have begun to consider how to start and finish your speech. Before you do this, you should plan the body of the speech (referred to under Preparing an Outline), which will help lead you to an introduction. The introduction should

1. *Capture the attention of the audience.* The introduction gets the audience ready for the body of the speech.
2. *Indicate the direction the speech will take.* This is done by stating the thesis sentence precisely.

The introduction also might include an **overview**. This is done by mentioning the main points of the speech simply and briefly.

The conclusion should summarize the content of the speech and contain no new information. It should make reference to the main points and the thesis.

Introductions and conclusions both focus audience attention on the thesis and its development via the body of the speech. These components of a speech are discussed in more detail in Chapter 6.

Preparing the Speaking Notes and Evidence

Extemporaneous speaking means speaking from carefully prepared notes. This is the type of delivery used in most public speaking and the type of speaking covered in this chapter. Extemporaneous speaking is not reading a speech that is entirely written out, nor is it memorizing a speech that was written out. Extemporaneous speaking is rehearsed but allows flexibility and adjustment *while speaking*.

Speaking Notes

Because of the nature of extemporaneous speaking, preparation of **speaking notes** is important. Speaking notes reflect the outline of the speech and contain a keyword outline of the material you wish to cover—a skeleton of the total outline developed for the speech. We recommend that speaking and evidence notes be written on 4" × 6" note cards, which are large enough to be handled easily when speaking. **Figure 3.1** illustrates a sample note card.

The speaking notes for the topic of identity theft could be developed on a single 4" × 6" note card, front and back. The note card contains relevant information from the entire outline, and it is complete enough to allow you to use your thought processes while speaking. The Arabic numerals on the right side of the sample note card correlate your speaking notes with evidence cards. Cross-numbering the two sets of notes ensure that the note cards will be in order when you are speaking.

Evidence Cards

Many of the speeches you give in class will require you to use material from non-original sources. **Evidence cards** provide a means of recording and using non-original information. A 4" × 6" note card is suggested for each piece of evidence used in the speech. For example, by looking at the speaking note card in **Figure 3.1**, you will see that the speaker used 10 separate pieces of evidence and 10 different note cards.

Figure 3.2 shows a sample evidence card, citing the source of the information and providing the information itself as a direct quote. The speaker includes a note to himself or herself about the primary source of the information. The evidence card has been coded with an Arabic numeral in the upper right corner that corresponds to the first element of substructure on the sample speaking note card in **Figure 3.1**. We encourage you to try to organize the note cards so you can instantly organize the information you need for a smooth, cohesive speech.

Practicing the Speech

Being well prepared and well practiced go hand-in-hand. We recommend that you practice even the briefest speech on three different levels.

1. PRACTICE THE SPEECH SILENTLY. Rehearsing the wording of the speech in this way allows you to recognize and modify certain words or phrases that seem inappropriate.

2. PRACTICE THE SPEECH WORDING ALOUD. This is different from actually practicing delivery. Practicing aloud enables you to see if you have trouble pronouncing or articulating any of the words in the speech. Thorough preparation helps you identify potential pitfalls so you can modify them.

3. PRACTICE ACTUALLY DELIVERING THE SPEECH. You may find a willing listener to time the speech and to note words or ideas that are unclear. This practice also allows you to "feel" the speech develop as a total exercise. The goal of practicing delivery is to have a strong, direct, yet conversational delivery mode. This delivery—extemporaneous—provides the best and most sincere link between the speaker and the audience. Practicing delivery aloud also allows you to hear and listen to yourself. Soon you will come to know your own strengths as a speaker.

Having carefully prepared and practiced the speech, you are ready to approach the audience for the first time in class. This is when all your preparation will pay off. A speech delivered extemporaneously with poise has a conversational tone and is flexible in that the speaker can "read" the feedback of the audience and make minor adjustments to the message during the speech.

Introduction
    I. Personal Information
    II. Identity Theft Problems

Body
    I. Criminal Activities
        A. Illegal Immigration   1
        B. Terrorism   2
        C. Medical Drugs   3
    II. Financial Fraud
        A. Goods and Services   4, 5
        B. Credit   6, 7
    III. Identity Cloning
        A. Cyber Stalking   8
        B. Concealment   9, 10

Conclusions
    I. Widespread Issues
    II. Identity Theft Problems

Figure 3.1 ♟ Sample Speaking Note Card for Identity Theft Speech

---

1

Department of Justice website, **http://www.justice.gov/criminal/fraud/websites/idtheft.html**, downloaded January 14, 2013.

With enough identifying information about an individual, a criminal can take over that individual's identity to conduct a wide range of crimes: for example, false applications for loans and credit cards, fraudulent withdrawals from bank accounts, fraudulent use of telephone calling cards, or obtaining other goods or privileges, which the criminal might be denied if he were to use his real name.

Figure 3.2 ♟ Sample Evidence Note Card for Identity Theft Speech

Summary

The major steps in speech preparation are the following:

1. Based on the audience (or assignment), choose the subject area.

2. Analyze the subject area to focus on the topic.

3. Phrase the thesis sentence.

4. Select the organizational pattern for the body of the speech.

5. Outline the main points of the body of the speech, and subdivide the main points.

6. Choose the forms of support from the research, and give credit for the evidence.

7. Plan the introduction and the conclusion.

8. Prepare speaking notes and evidence cards.

9. Practice wording and delivering the speech.

These steps should not be viewed as a recipe for success, but they do provide a helpful guide. The following chapters expand on these steps.

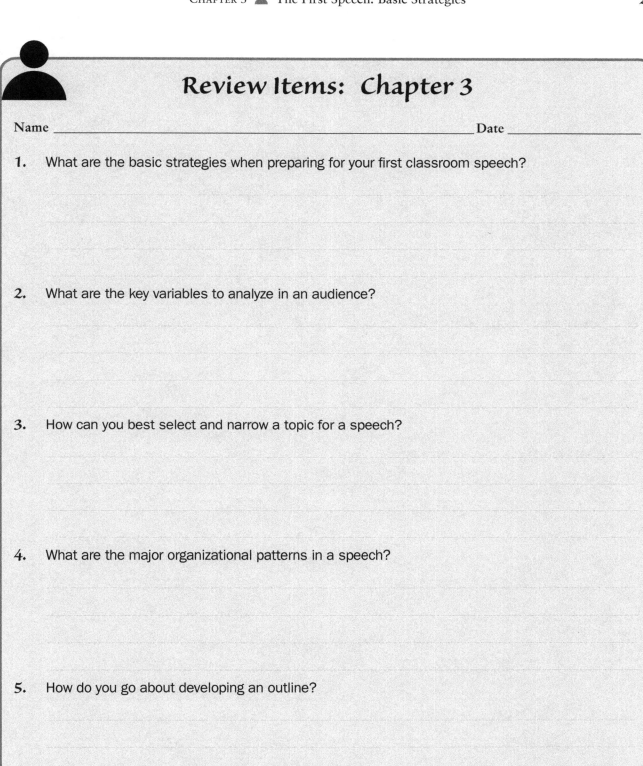

Review Items: Chapter 3

Name _____ Date _____

1. What are the basic strategies when preparing for your first classroom speech?

2. What are the key variables to analyze in an audience?

3. How can you best select and narrow a topic for a speech?

4. What are the major organizational patterns in a speech?

5. How do you go about developing an outline?

6. What types of support are available to a beginning speaker?

7. What are the characteristics of the introduction and the conclusion?

8. Explain speaking notes and evidence cards.

9. What are the three levels of practice?

1.

2.

3.

Listening Strategies

4

Your first speech would be fruitless without someone to listen to it—an audience. Your participation in this course includes the role of a listener to other speakers in a number of speaking situations. According to the International Listening Association (ILA), listening is the process of receiving, constructing meaning from, and responding to spoken and/or nonverbal messages (ILA, 1996).

You might be surprised at how much time you spend listening. According to the International Listening Association, U.S. college students spend anywhere from 24 percent to 55 percent of an average day engaged in listening behavior;[1] some estimates are even higher. This means that the other communication forms—speaking, reading, and writing—compete for about half of the time we communicate. If you are like most people, you probably spend at least as much time receiving communication as you do sending messages.

The Nature of Communication

Communication requires us to receive, process, and store messages more frequently than we produce them. During our waking hours we are bombarded with conversation, speeches, advertisements, and media presentations of all kinds. Much of the information we obtain from these messages may be useful (if not necessary) to us in the future. Effectiveness of our storage and retrieval system for this information depends mainly on listening. Your effectiveness as a speaker and an analyst is influenced strongly by listening habits and skills.

The Importance of Listening

How important is listening? Suppose a friend invited you to attend a concert by your favorite group. Your friend told you that the tickets had been purchased and that you would get a phone call to finalize the details. It just so happened that when you were called you were watching an interesting movie on TV, and you misunderstood when and where you were to meet your friend to get the tickets so you could attend the concert together. You showed up at what you thought was the appointed

---

1 International Listening Association (2008). *Listening Facts, Time Spent Listening and Communicating*. Retrieved February 8, 2008

time and place, but your friend wasn't there. If you had listened more carefully, your original plans would have been fulfilled.

Ineffective listening can have more disastrous effects than missing a concert. Good listening skills are required to assure accurately completing work instructions, correctly understanding and interpreting political messages, and responding to severe weather bulletins, for example.

The Citizen/Analyst Role

Developing and practicing effective listening skills may help you make the best voting choice, save your job someday—or even save your life. Listening skills are essential in our society. Your role as a citizen/analyst depends on them.

College students are in an ideal circumstance to learn and practice these skills in preparation for later roles as informed, active members of society. As a student in general, and a student in this class specifically, your speech communication responsibilities will include:

1. giving public speeches

2. critiquing the speeches of others

3. providing constructive feedback to others

A major portion of this text and of this course is devoted to learning and practicing the skills necessary for presenting prepared speeches. Much of a public speaker's success, however, comes from listening to and analyzing others' messages. The classroom is an ideal setting for learning and practicing listening skills. Your responsibilities in the speech class go well beyond giving speeches. Your feedback in class is important to the instructor and to your classmates, and feedback is based on effective listening.

When you leave the classroom, your listening responsibilities will continue, because the real world requires effective listening as well. In the public domain, responsible citizens have to be well informed to make judgments about public information, to interact with public information sources, and to act on public information.

Whether you are fulfilling your role as a student or as a citizen, four basic skills are required:

1. Understanding the speech communication process

2. Presenting information and opinions effectively

3. Listening to and critically evaluating information from a variety of sources

4. Taking action based on informed choices

The third of these skills is discussed in the remainder of this chapter.

The Listening Process

Many people believe that listening simply means sitting and absorbing what is going on around them and hoping that something will sink in. Passive listening occurs all the time, whether we are sitting in the student union on campus casually watching the latest sports news, overhearing a conversation in the hall as we walk to our next class, or turning on the TV when we are studying. Active listening is not that simple; it takes time and effort, because you are attempting to understand what another person is saying. The goal of active listening is to fully comprehend the messages being presented.

We use the term *process* to describe listening behavior. As this term implies, listening involves several stages, or phases:

1. Hearing

2. Attending

3. Understanding

4. Remembering

The **hearing** component seems obvious and is the process of picking up aural and/or visual stimuli. Those with hearing difficulties face an immediate barrier. If someone cannot hear normally then listening is impaired.

If you have ever felt hunger pangs during your late-morning classes, you know that **attending** to communication around you can be difficult. Our attention during lectures and conversation is easily diverted by a number of factors—loud noises, daydreaming, and room temperature, to name just a just a few. To attend well to a message, we have to make a choice to focus on the message, despite other stimuli in our environment.

Let's assume for a moment that you can hear the message and are attending to it without much difficulty. If you can't understand what is being said, though (assuming that the speaker is communicating well), you aren't listening effectively. Factors such as biases and a lack of familiarity with certain words or concepts often detract from actual **understanding**, although we may think we know what the message is about. It takes work to understand a message, to which every student can testify.

If we are excellent listeners but don't recall what we have heard, we have wasted this part of our listening skills. Many of us listen well but fall short in **remembering**. The trick to remembering is to evaluate the message and then process the message on an internal level. If your instructor is lecturing about the role of high blood sugar and diabetes, you will not only evaluate the information from your instructor and the sources of evidence the instructor uses, you may also internalize this information by thinking about a grandparent who is diabetic and has to control his or her intake of sugar.

The process of listening is complex, because as humans our messages are complex. Effective listening requires active participation, a focus on the message, and alertness.

Barriers to Effective Listening

Listening patterns become habitual. Therefore, poor listening habits become difficult for us to identify and even more difficult to change. Golen[2] listed the most predominant barriers to effective listening, as discussed below.

Faking Attention

People fake attention for a number of reasons. Perhaps we want to appear interested to please the speaker, or to prevent an instructor or speaker from developing a negative attitude toward us. Audience members might want to appear courteous and supportive of the speaker and his or her message.

Listening Only for Facts

When we listen only for facts, we do not listen for the speaker's main ideas. Students required to sit for long hours taking notes in the classroom may fall victim to this barrier. You may resort to writing down only the information you think you will be required to know for testing. This practice interferes with listening and also challenges learning, because a vital part of your education revolves around the need to identify ideas, formulate your own opinions, and think for yourself.

Avoiding Difficult Material

Listening to something we already understand or know is easy. Little mental or physical energy is required to absorb familiar messages. By contrast, difficult or unfamiliar material takes a great deal of energy. Common reactions to difficult material include boredom, restlessness, and sometimes frustration. As a result, we may avoid difficult listening situations by developing a casual attitude, by telling ourselves that the message is not important, or that we can learn it later. Perhaps this has happened to you during chemistry or math class—or even a speech class!

Avoiding the Uninteresting

If a listener perceives a message as uninteresting, even boring, it is easy to stop listening. The problem is that unconsciously (or consciously) we are making a judgment that this information is not important or valuable. If the message does not retain our interest, listening is not enjoyable, so we stop listening for messages that in reality might be important.

Criticizing the Speaker

Sometimes we become so wrapped up in the speaker and how the speech is delivered that we abandon the message totally to concentrate on its delivery. Accepting or rejecting what a speaker says based on how the message is presented violates the role of citizen/analyst. As a student, you might reject important information presented by professors and instructors based solely on the way they present the ideas.

Criticism of a speaker can go far beyond the way a speaker delivers his or her message. Our perception of speakers and their role or status also influences listening. If we are listening to a speaker we hold in high esteem, we may tend to accept all that is said without critically analyzing the message. If, however, we hold a speaker in low esteem, or if we perceive differences in status between us, we might tune out the speaker's message. Failing to acknowledge the legitimacy of the speaker or the ideas challenges the listening process.

Yielding to Distractions

Three categories of distractions—mental, semantic, and physical—can inhibit the listening process.

1. MENTAL DISTRACTIONS are internal. We allow ourselves to daydream, think about our plans for the weekend, or worry about an upcoming

2 "A Factor Analysis of Barriers to Effective Listening," by S. Golen, in *Journal of Business Communication*, 27 (1990), 25–36.

exam. Obviously, when this happens, we cannot listen effectively.

2. SEMANTIC DISTRACTIONS are those arising from differences in the meaning of words, phrases, or ideas. These distractions can be attributed to differences in culture, generations, or the use of jargon or **slang**. Semantic distractions can also be as simple as being introduced to words or concepts we have never heard of or don't understand. If you think about it that is what often happens in a college classroom! If listening is interrupted by a semantic distraction, the listener must stop and consider what the speaker means while the speaker is continuing his or her presentation.

3. PHYSICAL DISTRACTIONS tend to provide us with excuses for not listening carefully. Distractions can consist of a very warm classroom, a noisy heater, a loud conversation down the hallway, or the odor from a chemistry experiment. Perhaps you have listened to a speaker in a small, cramped room; or have attended services in a beautiful, ornate church; or have been assigned a seat in need of repair. Physical distractions can take many forms, and these distractions might assume more importance than what is being said by the speaker.

A number of other barriers to effective listening can interfere with our responsibilities as a citizen/analyst. As listeners, we sometimes find it convenient to filter the messages presented. This is another way of saying that we hear what we want to hear. For example, your speech instructor tells you that your next speech exam will be postponed for one week. In your excitement over the good news, you filter out the additional message that the postponed exam will cover one more chapter. On the day of the test, you are amazed and upset that you are not prepared to answer the questions pertaining to the additional material.

Or you may be listening to a campaign speech by a presidential candidate who informs the audience that there will be no additional tax increases during his or her administration. As a citizen, you welcome this piece of information, but you may have failed to listen to the follow-up message that because the candidate will forego additional taxes, cuts will be necessary in the national student loan program. By not listening to the total message, you have failed in your role as an analyst. It is important to listen for the

total message and resist the temptation to listen only for ideas and views that support your own beliefs.

Another way to inhibit the listening process is to simultaneously rehearse a response internally. In your speech class you will be listening to a number of topics, and views on these topics, throughout the course. Many of these topics will be controversial, and you may have strong convictions about some of them. Instead of listening carefully to a speaker and the total message, you might sit back and respond silently to ideas or arguments the speaker is making. This distraction obviously keeps you from attending to the message.

Or perhaps your instructor will comment about a topic you have chosen for an assignment, indicating that you should have narrowed this topic to better accommodate the assignment. You become defensive and stop listening to the suggestions your instructor gives you.

Finally, as listeners we tend to make inefficient use of the **speech/thought differential**. As speakers, we average 125–150 words per minute; however, we can think or mentally process approximately 400 words per minute. You can see why it is so easy to let our minds wander and allow internal or external distractions to take over. When this happens, our critical listening skills diminish.

Improving Listening Skills

Fortunately, poor listening habits can be overcome, and listening can be modified and improved. Sincere desire is necessary to improve communication skills. The college classroom, and in particular the speech course, offers the opportunity to develop better listening habits. Throughout the semester, you will hear a number of speeches on many different and exciting topics that will directly affect and inform you. Some specific suggestions and ideas for effective listening are presented in the following pages.

1. DEVELOP LISTENING OBJECTIVES FOR EACH SITUATION. Speakers will want to determine the purpose or objective for each speaking situation. This is true for listeners as well. By knowing the reasons for listening you will be better able to listen carefully and extract the information and response you desire from the speaker. When we listen to our favorite comedian on television, we are listening for entertainment. When we are attending church services, we are listening for

inspiration and guidance. When we tune into the evening news, we are listening for information about what happened in the world during the day in an attempt to stay current.

At times we listen so we may critically evaluate events, messages, and ideas. Certainly we do this when we attend a forum featuring candidates who are running for political office, or when we listen to insurance representatives discussing the options available with insurance policies.

As a citizen/analyst, you will have to determine what listening objectives pertain to each situation. Once you have identified these listening objectives, you will be able to determine your reasons and motives for listening to the message.

2. DEVELOP SKILLS OF CONCENTRATION. If you are tired, hungry, or upset, you will have difficulty listening and concentrating. Nevertheless, if you focus on the message rather than yourself or your surroundings and do not give in to distractions, you will find it easier to concentrate. Clear your mind and desk of everything, except perhaps paper and pen for note taking. Sit where you can hear and see without effort. Establish eye contact with the speaker, sit up straight, and attend to the message.

3. LISTEN FOR IDEAS, NOT JUST FACTS. Quite often when we listen, we get caught up trying to gather every specific piece of information the speaker offers. We are so busy listening for facts that we miss the speaker's general ideas. These general ideas may be just as important—if not more important—than the specific details.

An effective speaker develops a speech around a central idea and then uses several main points to build an organized message. This is where listening for ideas will benefit you. As a listener, identify the major points the speaker is covering. Assuming that the speaker uses overviews to present each major idea, it will be easy to follow the organization and understand the main points being made.

4. IDENTIFY AND EVALUATE SUPPORT MATERIAL FOR THE MAJOR IDEAS. After a speaker has given the main points of a message, listen for supporting evidence. Main ideas by themselves are only assertions. Evidence is required to make the claims valid. Basic questions to ask about a speaker's evidence include:

♟ Is the evidence current?

♟ Is the evidence taken from credible sources?

♟ Is the evidence comprehensive?

In Chapter 8 we will discuss these tests of evidence along with other evaluation techniques.

5. MENTALLY SUMMARIZE THE MAJOR IDEAS. Mentally summarizing and reviewing a speaker's main points is surprisingly easy. Remember the speech/thought differential? We think approximately three times faster than we speak; therefore, we have time available to think about what the speaker is saying. An alert listener can use this time to reinforce the speaker's message, eliminating the tendency to daydream and become distracted. You will reinforce what you already have heard and also will minimize the possibility of missing important information.

6. LISTEN FOR USEFUL INFORMATION. A skilled speaker will provide cues in the structure of a speech to ensure that the listening audience receives the message. Listen for overviews indicating the main ideas in the speech. Speakers, too, sometimes use transitions to indicate that they are moving on to a new idea. And summaries of information just covered reinforce the mental summaries that listeners have made. Repetition is another useful tool. When a speaker makes a point of reviewing an idea several times, perhaps in different ways, that message is worth remembering.

7. DON'T BE DISTRACTED BY LANGUAGE AND/OR DELIVERY. How often have we discounted a speaker's ideas because we are caught up with the way he or she dresses, sounds, or looks? We must suspend judgment about speakers and their message until *after* we have heard the total message. Although preconceived notions about people are difficult for most of us to ignore, this is one of the most important responsibilities you will face as a citizen/analyst. You must avoid tuning out a speaker simply because his or her language or delivery has a negative impact on you.

At the same time, be alert to the speaker who presents a positive image with a polished delivery and impeccable appearance. Just because a speaker projects a positive image does not mean that you should give merit to the speaker's message without evaluating its content and the speaker's motives.

8. PRACTICE EFFECTIVE LISTENING SKILLS. You will have the opportunity to practice the listening skills discussed in this chapter by virtue of your presence in a speech class and as a member of the college community. Take advantage of guest speakers and lecturers. Develop motivational patterns for yourself in each class you attend. Observe the speaking and listening patterns of your peers, instructors, and community leaders. The time and effort you devote to enhancing your listening skills will prepare you to become a better student/citizen/analyst and thereby reap immeasurable personal rewards.

Evaluation and Feedback

We listen for a reason. Usually we listen to gain information or to be entertained, but we also listen to form opinions or to evaluate. Evaluation is part of the process of providing feedback to the speaker. Although most of us do not comfortably evaluate our peers, either during conversation or when listening to speeches, we do evaluate in other ways. These ways may be subtle, such as avoiding interpersonal contacts with those we don't agree with; or they may be direct, such as voting for or against a candidate. These are examples of **evaluative feedback**.

Part of your development as a citizen/analyst is to refine your skills in evaluating public discourse. By the end of this course, you will have an expanded repertoire of knowledge about what constitutes good public speaking. The course also is designed to sharpen your skills as an analyst of public discourse. To develop as an analyst, you should be aware of how to give feedback.

General suggestions for giving feedback are:

1. Give descriptive feedback
2. Give feedback in specifics
3. Give feedback that is directed toward behaviors
4. Give feedback that is constructive

These suggestions apply directly to the process of speech criticism, which is evaluative. A speech, like a dance performance, can be compared to a standard. As a critic who is expected to evaluate, you can judge the speech against what you know about good speaking—the standards of strong rhetorical practice. In evaluating, you provide the speaker with feedback that deals with *specific behaviors* that he or she exhibited during the speech. Therefore, part of the analysis is *descriptive*. Because public speaking analysis is evaluative, however, we expect you to move from simply describing to comparing the speeches you hear to the standards of rhetorical practice. Thus, you evaluate in a way that extends feedback into **constructive evaluation**. As you work through learning strategies of rhetorical practice, you will come to understand evaluation more thoroughly.

Resources

To learn more about the listening process, check out the International Listening Association website, http://www.listen.org. This site provides professional information about the organization as well as links to listening resources, exercises, and material.

Summary

Listening is integral to communication. We tend to believe we can listen adequately because we can *hear* adequately. Often, however, our hearing is strong but our listening is weak. In addition to hearing, listening involves attending, understanding, and remembering.

Barriers to listening include faking attention, listening only for facts, tuning out difficult material, avoiding the uninteresting, criticizing the speaker, and yielding to distractions. These barriers can be overcome with training and practice.

One way to enhance listening behaviors is to learn to critique public speaking. This involves giving feedback and evaluating speeches according to the standards of rhetorical practice.

Review Items: Chapter 4

Name _____ Date _____

1. About how much of our communication time do we spend listening?

2. What are your major responsibilities as a listener?

3. What are the four stages of the listening process?

4. What are some barriers to effective listening?

5. In what ways can you improve your listening skills?

6. What is evaluative feedback? How should feedback be given?

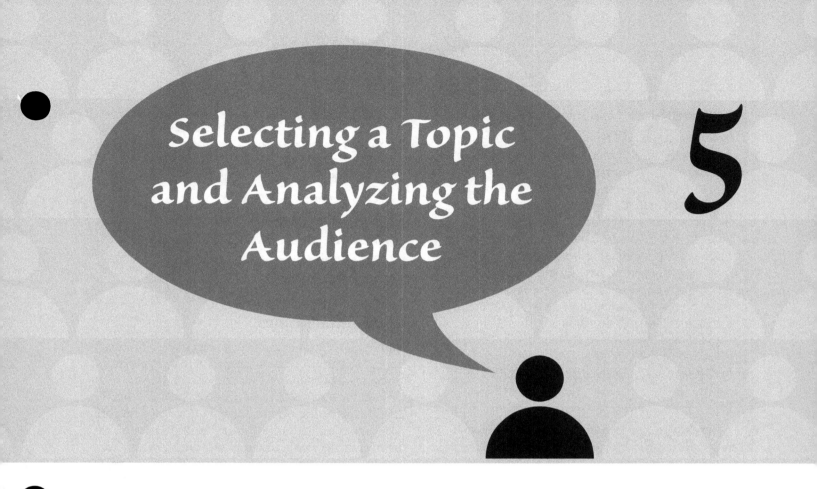

Selecting a Topic and Analyzing the Audience

5

The question that beginning speech students ask most often is: "What should I choose for a topic?" The answer to, and the problem with, that question is that the answer lies with the student. Speech instructors can guide, suggest, and challenge students to find appropriate topics, but the ultimate responsibility is up to the student. As a result, students often become frustrated when trying to select a topic. Choosing a topic is a major task, and in this chapter we discuss some ways to make that task easier. We also will explore important audience variables that can be analyzed so you can better develop a topic and prepare a speech.

Purpose of the Speech

In the classroom you will be given a clear assignment that indicates the purpose of the speech. For example, you may be told that your speech is to be informative or persuasive. These represent two different kinds of speeches that require two different approaches.

When you know the purpose of a speech, you have cleared a major hurdle. A key to selecting a topic is to know the purpose of the speech and adhere to it.

Personalizing a Topic

Many beginning speakers do not realize they have a lot to offer other people. A speech class is a good place to examine your experiences and develop topics that are familiar to you. Many things may seem too common to appeal to an audience, but proficient speakers are able to take "common" topics and creatively develop speeches from them.

Each of us has experience, knowledge, and beliefs that can help in the topic selection process. Beginning speakers should examine their experiences to see if any of them might be suitable for speeches. Students sometimes think their background is unimportant, that their personal experiences don't count. If you overcome this negative attitude, you will find that you have a wide range of potential topics from which to choose.

Example: Personalizing a Topic

One day in class I joked about my concern when my future husband was taking me to meet his parents for the first time. Because my future in-laws first language was not English, I worried about being able to effectively communicate with them during this first meeting. My husband laughed and encouraged me to just "smile and nod" and reassured me everything would be fine. As it turned out, he was right! This anecdote spurred a discussion in the class about initial interactions and cultural differences. As it turned out, one of the students in the class was an international student, and she decided to develop a speech on the differences in conversational norms between Western and Eastern cultures.

Developing a speech from a familiar topic has a major advantage: If you are interested in or enthusiastic about the topic, you probably will *demonstrate* that interest and enthusiasm in the speech. People enjoy listening to an excited and energetic speaker. As a speaker, you have to believe that what you are talking about is important and worth sharing. Your topic choice says a great deal about you, about how you feel about the topic, and the degree to which you value your audience members and their time and energy.

To get started on this process, two different lists are included as Appendix items. The first, Appendix A, is a personal inventory list for you to complete. It offers an opportunity to develop potential topics based on your personal experiences.

The second, Appendix B, is a personal brainstorming guide. **Brainstorming** means listing any and all ideas that come to mind. You don't have to evaluate the ideas or topics; just write down whatever pops into your mind. When you fill in this guide, think about topics you would like to investigate or learn more about. Both of these lists should help you select topics for different assignments.

Using the Media

If you still find yourself searching for possible speech topics, the media can provide many possibilities. First, stay current on world, national, and local events. Make it a habit to read daily newspapers.

Watch a news program for a few minutes every day. A number of 24-hour news networks provide coverage of current events on both television and the Internet. The Internet is also a valuable tool in searching for and researching topics. Some useful sites include:

- Google: www.google.com
- Yahoo!: www.yahoo.com
- Research Paper: www.researchpaper.com
- CNN Interactive: www.cnn.com
- Bing: www.bing.com

Unfamiliar Topics

Although we encourage students to rely on familiar topics, this may not be appropriate for all speeches. Some students develop excellent speeches from unfamiliar topics. Don't be afraid to talk to others; find out what they are interested in. As you generate ideas, bounce them off of your friends to gauge interest or develop additional ideas. It's possible to speak about scientific and technological advancements, social phenomena, or government problems without having any personal experience with them. If any of these subjects arouse your interest, a speech topic may be there waiting to be developed. Interest in a topic is a good substitute for experience.

Constraints

The public speaker is constrained by several factors. One, discussed earlier, is the purpose of the speech. Other major limitations are time and information.

Time

In any public speaking class you will face deadlines. Your instructor usually allows plenty of time to complete assignments, but you must balance the time spent picking a topic with time spent developing the speech. Topic selection is important, but you must complete this task rather quickly because of the overall deadline.

In a speech assignment, the time limits for the speech are made clear. You surely can recall speeches that were long and boring or short and sweet. What do you remember about Sunday sermons? Sometimes audience comments relate to length of time, not content.

Say you have been assigned a six-minute speech and are interested in the events surrounding the turmoil in the Middle East. It would be impossible to cover the historical, ethnic, political, religious, and economic implications that have led to unrest over the centuries in this part of the world. Time is a limiting factor.

If you keep time in mind when selecting topics, your speeches will become more workable. We will look at topic selection as a beginning step. Then you will be asked to develop strategies for focusing or narrowing the topic.

Information

Nearly every speech you deliver in a beginning speech course will be based on research of some sort. When selecting a topic, you must consider the amount of information available for a research base. In Chapter 7 the research process is examined at length.

Even though you choose a good topic, it may be so new that information is not readily available through traditional research resources found in print and libraries. The Internet and other electronic sources now make researching speech topics easier and information more accessible. You have online access in your residence hall or at home. Your college or university is connected to the Internet. Your library encourages access to its electronic databases and the Internet. We encourage you to search online. We do, however, offer a word of caution: "Surfing the net" can be so much fun that the purpose of an online search might get lost! And because sources are not always subject to the usual scrutiny, you will have to determine which are credible.

Immediately after you have selected a topic for a speech, you should begin your research to see if you can obtain sufficient information on the topic. Knowing that enough research is available will allow you to continue your speech preparation.

Selecting a speech topic is a frequent stumbling block for students. As you learn more speech preparation strategies, though, selecting a topic should become easier. Some of those strategies will be analyzed in this chapter and others in later chapters.

Analyzing the Audience

The **audience** must be the focus of your message; it is the sole purpose for the speech presentation. In some audiences you might know one or more persons who hold certain views about a topic. This knowledge will give you an idea about what strategies to use to effectively communicate with those you know. More likely, however, the audience will be a collection of people you don't know very well. In this case, audience analysis is essential. As introduced in Chapter 3, variables to be identified in an audience include, but are not limited to, age, gender, cultural composition, size of the audience, educational level, occupation or profession, informational sources, and expectations.

Age

A college class is likely to be composed mostly of people of the same general age. The average age in college classes is just above the average high school graduation age. However, it's becoming common to find "nontraditional" students, those who have either deferred their college education for a few years or are returning to campus to resume their education.

Communicating with people of different ages requires you to alter your public speaking strategies. You wouldn't talk to your parents or grandparents the same way you talk with your siblings or friends. Age does make a difference. In some speaking situations age varies widely within the same group. If you fail to consider age differences when preparing your speech, you might exclude some audience members from your message.

Gender

Despite our view of equality between the sexes, we still must shape our speeches according to the gender composition of the audience. Unless you are speaking to an all-female audience or a male-only audience, choosing a topic that has no appeal to most males or to most females will alienate a large proportion of your audience.

Example: Analyzing the Audience

One class was composed of 14 males and 5 females. In addition, many of the men were agriculture and biological science majors. One of the female students used this gender imbalance strategically in her speech. She chose a topic that would relate to the men in her class...the shrinking numbers of family-owned farms and ranches in the country. The majority of these farms and ranches are traditionally passed down from grandfathers and fathers to sons, but the numbers are in decline. In the speech, she analyzed the topic from the point of view of what could be done to salvage the family farm. She was able to find a topic that the men in the class could relate to and argued that family farms also need to be passed down to daughters, thus making the topic relevant to the women in the class.

Cultural Composition

The United States is a diverse society. Our strength as a nation depends on working together to solve problems. Often, though, this **diversity** causes problems. A speech course offers an opportunity to analyze issues of diversity to promote harmony. As a speaker, you must consider audience members who are not like you. Diversity studies, popular in U.S. universities, often include cultural and gender issues—factors that also are important in developing public speaking strategies.

Size of Audience

Generally, your speech class audience will be about the same from speech to speech. In other situations you will want information about the size of your audience beforehand so you can consider and plan the physical facilities for the speech. For a large audience you may need a public address system. If you are using audio or visual aids, planning depends upon the number of people in the audience.

Educational Level

You may want to analyze the educational level of the audience. If your audience is like you—university students—your task may be easy. But even a speech class can represent different educational levels. As more nontraditional students enter college, you may have classmates with college degrees, technical degrees, or work experiences equivalent to years of formal education. Speech classes commonly include students with these varied experiences.

Educated audiences have been shown to be more critical than those with less education.[1] If you have an educated audience, you often must construct a speech that anticipates the criticisms. Knowing the educational level of your audience will make your task easier.

Occupation or Profession

Audiences might be represented by various occupations or professions. Classroom speakers sometimes refer to things they think everyone in the audience will relate to. For example, a speaker might discuss teenage employment situations (fast food, for example). To assume that the entire audience is familiar with and interested in these occupations can be faulty.

Informational Sources

The public speech normally is built on a strong foundation of research or information from other than personal sources. We do not trust all sources, and it stands to reason that a speech based on weak informational sources will lack impact. Therefore, the speaker will have to discover what sources the audience considers credible.

Expectations

The audience will know the purpose of the speech, as assigned by the instructor. If the expectations of purpose are not met, the audience might be thrown off. Further, audiences expect speeches to fit within a time frame or assignment limitations. If you are to give a five-minute informative speech, the audience may lose interest or become restless if the speech is longer or strays from the informational limitation.

Additional Variables

To the above audience variables we add:
- *geographic area(s)* represented in the group
- *economic status* of audience members
- *predominant concerns* of the audience
- *sexual orientation* of the audience members
- *religious affiliations* represented in the audience
- *political affiliations* represented in the group

---

1   B.E. Bradley, *Fundamentals of Speech Communication: The Credibility of Ideas*, 5th ed. (Dubuque, Iowa: W. C. Brown, 1988), 337–338.

As you become more familiar with your classmates, you will realize how important some of these variables are. In many audiences, however, you will have to discover this additional information. Through audience analysis, you will learn about the homogeneity or heterogeneity of the group. A good speaker tracks common ground in an audience and develops a speech based on audience experiences and your analysis.

From Topic Selection to Speech Preparation

After you have gained a thorough knowledge of the audience, you can embark on speech preparation. Each step in this process builds upon the others, and each contributes to the success of the others. To reiterate, these steps are:

1. Know the purpose of the speech
2. Know the limitations imposed for the speech
3. Know the limitations imposed by materials available for the speech
4. Know the audience

Now you can begin constructing the thesis.

Constructing the Thesis

The step of developing a thesis sentence was introduced in Chapter 3. Proper phrasing of the thesis can turn a broad, unrestrained topic into a focused, constrained subject for a speech. Without a properly phrased thesis, the speaker has free rein to amble without direction.

The first requirement is that the thesis must be *a complete declarative sentence*. Students often erroneously use a question as the thesis. In our approach to speech, the question is answered by phrasing the thesis properly. A declarative sentence clearly states the constraints placed on a topic.

Suppose you want to speak about mental health resources. To begin analyzing the topic, you ask the question:

How can we provide mental health services to everyone who needs them?

The question limits the topic somewhat but not significantly. Your research should provide several answers, including expansion of diagnostic services, more mental health-care providers, and expanded insurance coverage of mental health services. Your research also might direct you to the increased need for mental health care for young children and adolescents. As you can see, your topic is still extremely broad—too broad to develop each idea in a classroom speech.

If you develop just one of these ideas, however, and phrase it as a declarative sentence, the thesis could read:

Increased insurance coverage for mental health services will expand the availability of mental health care.

This thesis clearly limits or constrains what will be presented in the speech. The broad topic of mental health has been narrowed significantly.

Stating the thesis as a declarative sentence rather than as a question aids speech preparation, because you have provided a clear direction and focus for the speech. Phrasing the thesis as a declarative sentence also allows you to meet the second requirement of a proper thesis: *The thesis must contain the central idea of the speech*. This sounds simple, but if the thesis is not phrased properly, the audience will not realize the central idea of the speech. The declarative sentence should state the main idea clearly.

The third requirement is that *the thesis sentence must demonstrate the purpose of the speech*. An audience member should be able to determine from the phrasing of the thesis that the speech is either informative or persuasive. By looking at the above thesis, you should conclude that it is informative. By contrast, a persuasive thesis on the same topic might be phrased:

The federal government should provide incentives for insurance companies to expand mental health-care coverage.

Each thesis indicates the direction of the speech, or the response the speaker seeks. Each specifies the purpose clearly.

Last, *the thesis should be phrased in a way that gives direction to the body of the speech*. You may organize the body of the speech through the wording of the thesis. The thesis we have used in this example shows what the body of the speech will cover. An alternative thesis—*Access to mental health care is limited*—does not offer as much direction as the other thesis does.

Proper wording of the thesis is vital to a speech. It limits the speech. It focuses research and organization and serves as a focal point for the audience.

Summary

The speech preparation process requires making strategic choices, beginning with selecting the topic. Topic selection is influenced by the time available for the speech, by the purpose of the speech, by assignment limitations, and by the composition of the audience.

An analysis of your audience will increase the chances of the audience accepting your ideas. By taking into account the composition of the audience—including the variables of age and sex, economic status, geographical representation, and others—you will be a more effective speaker.

Speeches are given for a purpose. The people represented in the audience and what they want to hear are vital concerns. Your strategic choices as a speaker are constrained by knowledge of the audience.

When the audience and topic are known, major steps in preparing a speech have been accomplished. Phrasing a proper declarative thesis sentence acknowledges the audience and purpose and gives you a focal point for developing the body of the speech.

Review Items: Chapter 5

Name _____ Date _____

1.   Explain the relationship between the purpose of a speech and the speech topic.

2.   Identify experiences you have had that might make good speech topics.

3.   What constraints do speakers face when choosing topics?

4.   Why is gender an important audience variable to consider when choosing a topic?

5.   Why is the audience's educational level important to a speaker?

6. What basic limitations should you consider when developing a topic?

7. What are the key requirements for a strong thesis statement?

The Speech Organization

6

One thing that surprises students in a basic speech course is the requirement to provide outlines of assigned speeches. Typically, these outlines are due on the day a student is required to present his or her speech. We hear comments like, "Why do I need an outline if this is a speech class?" Outlines are a necessary step in the process of creating a speech for several reasons. First and foremost, speakers need to have a way to organize their thoughts and information. Without some organizational structure, a speaker is likely to fail in his/her presentation. Ideas and information are likely to be scattered and not make sense. Second, an audience accepts and retains the messages in a speech much more readily when it is well organized because it will be easy to understand and follow. The task of organizing a speech requires selecting one of several ways to structure the body of the speech, developing the main points and their subordinate structure, and preparing the introduction and conclusion. In addition to covering these patterns, this chapter presents the standards of proper outlining, as well as transitions and overviews.

Organizational Patterns

The body of the speech is composed of main points supported by subpoints, which in turn are supported by evidence (discussed in Chapter 8) or by your analysis. A major task in speech preparation is to select the method of structuring the main points that best conveys your message to the audience. This means choosing an organizational pattern for the body of the speech.

The body of the speech proves the thesis, and your strategies for proving the thesis include the organizational structure of the speech. Four general patterns that are used for organizing the body of the speech are: topical, spatial, chronological, and logical. The first three are used in informative speaking. The logical organization pattern is used in problem/solution speaking.

Topical Organization

The **topical pattern** is one of the most common ways to organize the body of a speech. In this organization the body of the speech is arranged according to subject matter. If you are preparing a speech for which the topic or thesis does not suggest another organizational pattern, a topical organizational pattern likely will work.

Suppose the thesis of the speech is:

There are differences between performing community service and volunteering.

You quickly realize that the thesis imposes a requirement on the structure of the speech: You must have two main points. For example:

I. Community service is often a mandatory activity.

II. Volunteering is considered a selfless act that is not required.

The first main point does not have to refer to community service. This could have been the last point. The topical pattern simply provides a structure by which the key subject matter and subtopics support the thesis. Any of the main points could be first, and any could be last.

This organizational pattern is the most versatile way to structure the body of a speech. It allows you to select the main points you wish to cover in the speech. The topical pattern allows you to make strategic choices. These choices enhance audience adaptation, enable you to narrow the topic and meet time constraints, and enable you to best prove the thesis.

Suppose the thesis is:

Gun control legislation is a complex, controversial, and difficult process.

The following main points could support this thesis:

I.   Gun control legislation has always been a complex issue.

II. Gun control legislation is very controversial in the United States.

III. Securing fair and appropriate gun control legislation is difficult.

These points allow you to explain and inform what the relevant issues are regarding gun control in the United States. Again, the first main point need not be first or last. The topical pattern allows a variety of strategic choices in structuring the body of a speech.

Spatial Organization

The **spatial pattern** is a geographical or locational one. It tells us that something is in a certain place. Descriptions of places and structures often are organized using this pattern. For example, a speech about the marine life of an ocean might follow the spatial pattern. First, you could show what marine life thrives in the epipelagic, or sunlight zone, of the ocean. Second, you could focus on marine life in the mesopelagic, or twilight zone. The third area of marine life is found in the bathypelagic, or midnight

zone. Marine life is then found in the abyssopelagic zone. You could complete the body of the speech by discussing the hadalpelagic zone, where only tiny, single-celled organisms can survive. The pattern is spatial, by geographical location.

The university setting is a good example to use for spatial organization. If you ask an instructor to describe university services available in the administration building, the response might well be spatial. He or she could describe service offices on the main floor, the second floor, and the third floor. This organizes the body of the speech by place.

Or you could develop a speech that discusses the changes in the ethnic population distribution in the United States. This speech could be organized spatially and explain the ethnic population increases and decreases in the regions of the country.

Although these examples illustrate spatial organization, the same topics could be developed using a topical pattern. The spatial pattern, however, does lend itself to organizing certain topics.

When selecting patterns, if a topical pattern seems to be effective, check to see if the spatial pattern would work just as well or better. A good public speaker recognizes which organizational pattern is best for the audience and the situation.

Chronological Organization

In the **chronological pattern** the body of the speech follows a time sequence. The chronological pattern is used most often in a **process speech**, which describes how something is done. Process speeches necessarily follow a specific order. If you have experience in developing a Facebook page, creating a website, raising cattle, or starting a weight loss program, you know the importance of following the proper sequence. The following example not only demonstrates what should be included on a resume but also shows the order in which information should occur:

There are five key sections to include on a resume.

You quickly realize that the thesis imposes a requirement on the structure of the speech: You must have five main points; also, the implication is that this speech will follow an order for where to include resume items. For example:

I. First, you must include your contact information on a resume.

II. An employment objective should be listed second.

III. The next section of the resume is the experience section.

IV. The fourth section of a resume should document your educational experiences.

V. The final section of a resume is the skills section.

The chronological pattern also could be used to show the sequence in which some historical event occurred. You could chart the development of online academic courses by looking at the time frame in which it happened; or something as simple as a report on your study abroad experience may follow the chronological pattern.

Like the other patterns, the chronological pattern may be interchanged with another organization. For example, a study abroad experience can be described spatially or topically, as could online academic courses.

Topical, spatial, and chronological organizational patterns are used extensively in informative speaking. They seem to have greater utility in imparting information than in persuading, to which the logical organizational pattern is applicable.

Logical Organization

The **logical pattern** is used in problem/solution speaking, commonly referred to as persuasive speaking. We will fully analyze this form of speech organization in Chapter 12. Briefly, it structures the speech by

1. analyzing the problem,

2. presenting a detailed solution, and

3. justifying the solution.

The first step may contain an analysis both of problems and their causes, depending on the situation. By thoroughly analyzing the problem and offering a detailed, justified solution you are able to influence the audience.

In this text we concentrate on a single persuasive pattern—the logical structure—although the other patterns mentioned will work in some persuasive situations. Whatever pattern you use, problem/solution speaking is essential in your role as a citizen/analyst.

Being aware of the structural choices available will increase the strategies at your disposal in preparing a speech. Other, more specialized organizational patterns are available, too. The four introduced here, however, are sufficient to know at this point.

Preparing Speech Outlines

For some reason, most of us don't like to prepare outlines, and students resist writing outlines or fail to properly develop outlines for speeches. Yet, outlining is an essential step in preparing for a public speech. The **outline** gives final structure to your thoughts and is integral to the speech itself. Certain principles of outlining guide the preparation of anything that requires structure. You might find these discussed in a writing class as well, because the principles are the same.

Six general criteria for outlining apply to all types of speeches, whether the message is to inform or to persuade: simplicity, coordination, subordination, symbolization, progression, and discreteness. Heeding these criteria will enhance your outlining and will help you create a speech structure that will have the greatest impact on your audience.

1. SIMPLICITY. Outline elements should be stated simply. Each unit (sentence) in the outline should contain only one idea. More than one idea will confuse the issues being analyzed in the speech. The following sentence fails in this regard:

   College internships are a smart choice for students because they can provide experience, on-the-job training, can eventually lead to a job offer, and make you stand out among the competition in job searches, but they take a lot of hard work and extra resources and the competition is great.

Consider this alternative:

I. Internships are beneficial for college students.

   A. Internships provide experience.

   B. On-the-job training is one advantage of an internship.

   C. Some students are offered jobs after graduation.

II. Internships are not always easy to secure.

   A. Internship placement takes a great deal of effort.

   B. Not all internships are paid.

   C. The process for awarding internships is very competitive.

      1. More and more students are applying for internships.

      2. Internships are becoming more demanding in terms of the specific skills interns are expected to possess.

The second example contains the same points as the first one. The second, however, illustrates a simple structure that would be easy to follow and expand upon in the speech.

2. COORDINATION. To be coordinated, a common thread must unite elements in an outline. This means that you should exclude unrelated ideas, for example:

I. There are a number of alternative energy sources.
   A. Wind energy is a growing source of energy.
   B. Solar energy taps the strength of the sun.
   C. Alternative energy sources will strengthen our economy.

The last element doesn't belong under the main point. Although it fits the general topic of alternative energy sources, it refers to the economy rather than the main point, energy sources.

3. SUBORDINATION. A proper outline is not simply a list of sentences that relate to a topic. It is a coordinated set of points and subpoints that relate to one another in a subordinate–superior relationship. The previous structure illustrates subordination. Note that the second main point is not subordinate to the first main point but the subpoints are subordinate to the main point. The proper structure for an outline is represented in the following.

I. Main point. (supports the thesis)
   A. Subpoint. (supports I)
   B. Subpoint. (supports I)
      1. Subpoint. (supports B)
      2. Subpoint. (supports B)
         a. Subpoint. (supports 2)
         b. Subpoint. (supports 2)

4. SYMBOLIZATION. The outline above shows the ranking of the outline elements in the standard outline form. The substructure can be developed even further, but the idea is clear. We have found that a speech develops more extemporaneously and is based on stronger analysis if your final outline is not more detailed. The finished speaking outline in this text should contain only main points and the first level of subpoints (A and B above), supported with evidence and analysis.

5. PROGRESSION. Adhering to the criterion of progression means that the ideas in an

outline follow a natural or logical sequence. In analyzing some ideas, the speech follows a chronological pattern. In such a speech you would not reverse steps in the process. Applying this criterion to outlining, you would put each step in its normal order. This text was developed following a logical progression. Thus, selecting a topic is discussed before outlining.

6. DISCRETENESS. Being discrete means that points in the outline do not overlap. Each point is a separate and distinct idea. This example illustrates lack of discreteness:

I. Social media opportunities exist in many forms.
   A. Facebook and Twitter are popular forms of social media.
   B. YouTube is a unique form of social media.

The first subpoint contains two ideas that could be separated to develop discrete ideas. It would be a simple matter to have three subpoints.

Again, all outline elements should be in sentence form. From sentences you can communicate complete ideas. Sentences provide boundaries or constraints. Let's look at an example that does not use sentences.

I. Environmental considerations
   A. Climate change
   B. Alternative energy sources

This outline tells you little. It might work as a beginning point for preparing a speech. Beyond that, it does little to structure your ideas. A better outline, using complete sentences, would be:

I. Our environment is experiencing significant challenges.
   A. Climate change is harming our environment.
   B. Alternative energy sources have not been effectively introduced.

These ideas are complete and can be substantiated with evidence and analysis.

The Introduction and the Conclusion

Although we concentrate on developing the body of the speech because it proves the thesis and is the focus of any argument you are making, outlining principles apply to the whole speech, including the introduction and conclusion. These form the important beginning and ending of a speech.

The Introduction

The body of the speech is prepared first so you can prove the thesis. After completing the body of the speech, you can develop the introduction. The introduction has two major functions.

First, *the introduction must get the attention of the audience*. Without gaining attention from the outset, the speech is likely to fail. In a speech on the use of the Internet an introduction might be phrased this way:

> Our lives have been transformed since the creation of the Internet. Because of the Internet, we have access to news and information in a matter of seconds. We have the capability to communicate and interact with family and friends in real time, even though we may be separated by hundreds and thousands of miles. Our capacity for learning and obtaining knowledge is limitless because of the Internet. However, every time we connect to the Internet hundreds of potential dangers are just a click away. (At this point you state the thesis.)

This introduction probably will gain the attention of at least some of the audience members, because they can relate to it. One of the most critical strategies a speaker should use is trying to connect or link the topic of the speech to the audience. Your goal is get the audience members attention and make them feel that what you have to say is important or interesting for them personally. The introduction should prepare the audience to listen to the remainder of the speech.

Once you gain the audience's attention, you should present the second crucial element of the introduction: *The introduction must state the thesis sentence precisely*. From the example above, you could use this thesis:

> There are untold dangers that exist when we connect to the Internet.

This element of the introduction consists of a precise statement of the thesis. The thesis sentence must be precise because the body of the speech depends on it to prove the thesis.

The introduction prepares the audience to receive the message. The introduction should be attractive, not distractive. For this reason, the introduction should avoid "cute" things such as jokes that don't relate to the subject, or other material that might distract the audience from the point of the speech, the thesis.

We also discourage using a **rhetorical question** in the introduction. This is a question for which an answer is not expected. If a rhetorical question is used, two things may happen:

1. A member of the audience might answer the question—creating a distraction for you to contend with.

2. A rhetorical question might encourage the audience to begin an analysis that is counter to the idea you will be offering in the speech.

In either case, rhetorical questions invite distractions.

When actually delivering the introduction, the first impression of the speaker is his or her physical image. Because the speaking condition naturally produces some anxiety, the speaker is likely to hurry into the content of his or her presentation. This often results in both the speaker and the audience being physically unprepared for the message.

For best results in the introduction, the speaker should approach the podium, face the audience, and wait briefly before beginning the speech. A brief period of silence at the podium signals the audience that the speaker is composed and about to begin. It also clearly establishes the speaker's physical presence in the room. The speaker can use the moments at the podium, without actually speaking, to calm him- or herself. This can be a time of reflection, of building inner confidence.

The Conclusion

At the end of a speech, the speaker makes a final impression on the audience. The conclusion provides an opportunity to end the speech on a positive note. It reiterates the thesis and the main points, leaving the audience with the major ideas contained in the speech.

A conclusion should not offer new arguments in support of the thesis. Introducing new evidence or analysis in the conclusion extends rather than ends the analysis that properly belongs in the body of the speech. A strong, positive conclusion reinforces the major thoughts of the speech for the audience.

Just as the introduction requires the attention of the audience, so does the conclusion. It's fine to state that the conclusion is coming. Speakers also should change their tone and stance to indicate to the audience that the conclusion is forthcoming.

Some students verbally announce the conclusion but fail to verify it physically. At the other extreme, some students actually move from the podium to their desk before ending the speech. This signals a lack of confidence to the audience.

Introductions and conclusions lead the audience into and out of speeches, respectively. For maximum effectiveness, both elements must demonstrate the positive attitude of the speaker toward the audience and the process.

Transitions

A transition is a statement that summarizes the main point you are concluding and forecasts the main point you are beginning. In short, **transitions** link major ideas in a speech. They are connections developed orally to enhance retention of the speaker's ideas. Although these transitions might not appear on paper (on the outline), they are vital to a speech.

Students typically fail to plan or prepare transitions. Beginning speakers often move between main points without leading the audience from one point to another. This can create a stressful speaking experience, because when a student presents a speech he or she may become "stuck" trying to move from one point to another. Suppose the first two main points of a speech are:

I. Society's view of attention deficit disorder has changed.

II. Attention deficit disorder is easily confused with other diseases.

A transition could be developed to link these two main points.

> The evidence shows that our society has changed how it thinks about attention deficit disorder. *Despite this change,* attention deficit disorder still is confused with other diseases.

This transition is simple, yet it links the main points and leads the audience from one point of analysis to the next. Without oral movement, the analysis lacks clarity. Transitions help the speech flow smoothly and give the audience members an opportunity to review what was just discussed while guiding them to the next area of discussion.

No hard and fast rules govern transitions. Often, simple, single words such as *next, furthermore, first, second,* and *finally* will suffice. Other transitions might be phrases such as:

The second point…

   In addition to…

      Another reason…

         An example of this is….

Keep in mind that transitions do not appear in the outline and usually are not included in the speaker's note cards. Nevertheless, they are fundamental to a well-delivered speech, and you must incorporate transitions in your rehearsal process.

The Overview

An **overview** is a statement usually given immediately after the statement of the thesis that forecasts the major points of analysis to be covered in the body of the speech. The overview helps the audience follow the speech as it develops, and it helps the audience identify the main points as they unfold. Coupled with strong transitions, overviews provide oral cohesion that enhances audience retention of the message.

Summary

The proper arrangement of ideas is necessary to make a speech acceptable and meaningful to an audience. The body of the speech can be organized in one of four patterns: (a) chronological or time; (b) spatial or geographical; (c) topical, which organizes the speech by subject matter; or (d) logical or problem/solution, best used with persuasive speeches.

Outlining enhances the structure of a speech. A proper outline puts order to thoughts. With a sentence outline you can see your ideas take form on paper. Your speech will benefit from a strong structure. The six outlining criteria that apply to all kinds of speech are: simplicity, coordination, subordination, symbolization, progression, and discreteness.

The introduction of a speech must gain the audience's attention, and the conclusion should summarize the main ideas without offering new points. Keeping the audience's attention at the beginning and ending of the speech will enhance acceptance and retention of the ideas presented in the speech. Finally, a good speech includes transitions and overviews.

Review Items: Chapter 6

Name _____ Date _____

1. What does the term *organization* mean in connection with preparing a speech?

2. What are the four major organizational patterns explained in this chapter?

3. What are six criteria to be applied to outlining?

    1.
    2.
    3.
    4.
    5.
    6.

4. Explain the standard system used in outlining.

5. Why does this chapter place so much emphasis on outlining the body of the speech?

6. What are the major requirements of a strong introduction?

7. What are the requirements of a conclusion?

8. What things should you consider when introducing and concluding a speech?

9. What is a transition?

10. What is an overview?

Researching the Speech

7

At the college level you are expected to do research for most of your speeches. In fact, almost any public speech should be based on research. The research aspect of a speech is not an extra step or an extra requirement placed on you to force you to use the library and other sources! As you listen to speeches, you will find that elected officials, professors, civic officials, and leaders of business and industry have researched their topics and use the research to bolster their claims. Using research to support your claims makes you more believable to audiences. For informative and persuasive speaking, especially, research is necessary.

In Chapter 3 we examined the process of moving from general thoughts about topics to phrasing purpose statements to completing a specific thesis sentence. The thesis sentence narrows a topic considerably, giving direction to the body of the speech. When researching a topic, the best strategy is to concentrate on your thesis. Often, however, you will have to do some research to find information that will help you phrase the thesis. At this point we view **research** as a search to find evidence to support your arguments, primarily those in the substructure of the body of the speech.

Basic Requirements of Research

When evaluating materials, three basic criteria apply.

1. Good research is CURRENT. Unless you are giving a speech with a historical perspective, the audience will expect the speech to be based on the latest research. Speech instructors often hear students make claims of "now" in their speeches while supporting those claims with evidence that is not current. There is no magical way to determine what is most current. One of the best approaches is to begin your search in the present and work backward. In doing so, you will access the most recent materials available.

2. Strong research comes from CREDIBLE sources. To determine exactly which information sources an audience will trust, you have to make some judgments about **credibility**. At a basic level, the source of information must be believable. We all know sources of information we don't trust. You wouldn't use these sources to support your ideas, even if they contain material you need. You should be wary of sources with obvious bias. These sources are plentiful, and they can be strong sources if you are giving a one-sided speech. The audience, however, is likely to

question these sources, especially if any members of the audience hold opposing views. Like so many other variables in public speaking, credibility of sources depends on others' perceptions. A good speaker uses research sources designed to leave a favorable impression with the audience.

3. Adequate research is COMPREHENSIVE. The scope, breadth, or depth of research should be sufficient to convince an audience that the main questions about the topic have been answered. This point is subjective, though, because one audience member might consider the research to be thorough enough and another may not.

When researching topics, keep these criteria in mind, because audience members make judgments about topics, speeches, and speakers based on the research materials cited.

Focusing on the Thesis

After you have phrased the thesis sentence, general research may enhance general knowledge about the subject, but it may not be sufficient to prove the thesis. Therefore, research should be specific and applicable to the thesis. Some research may be done to prepare for writing the thesis sentence, but the most thorough research should focus on the thesis after it has been written.

Using Personal Experience

We may have an interesting hobby or have extensive experience as an athlete; we may have had the opportunity to travel extensively overseas; or we may be interested in a specific academic major, such as physical therapy, because a friend had to spend time rehabilitating from an accident. Personal interest in a topic is bound to make a speech better. Although we might be critical of a speech based solely on personal experience, we also recognize that an individual's personal experience is valuable in public speaking. Using yourself as part of the foundation for a speech is a useful strategy.

One of my students gave a speech about the Humane Society. In this informative speech she described the process of how the Humane Society cares for and finds homes for abandoned and rescued pets. She used strong research throughout the speech and backed her claims thoroughly. It was a good speech, but this student failed to mention

anywhere in the speech that she was a longtime volunteer at the Humane Society. Her credibility certainly would have been enhanced had she backed it up with personal experience.

Using Personal Experience

For one speech assignment, students were instructed to express an attitude, supporting it with reasons they believe the way they do. One of the students, throughout his speech, referred to his own experiences working as a lifeguard and swim instructor. This aspect of his experience supported his claims about the necessity for and rewards of becoming a certified lifeguard.

Using Outside Resources

Giving good speeches requires you to draw from all the resources at your disposal. This includes outside research to support the claims made in the speech. Many of us think of research as using the library to find books about our topic or to locate relevant magazine or journal articles. This certainly is part of good research, but it is just one of many forms of outside research.

Listening/Viewing Resources

To many of us, television and radio simply provide entertainment. For students, though, these resources can be an important source of research. We pay attention to international, national, and local issues and concerns. We learn about weather patterns. We have access to original governmental hearings and similar proceedings through television's C-Span. Major listening/viewing sources are credible and can be broadly classified as news broadcasts and informational programming, documentary specials, and special programming.

News Broadcasts

By nature, radio and television news is more current than other "news." News broadcasts, especially those that provide in-depth coverage, typically contain research information. With the advent of 24/7 cable news programming, competition is more intense, so the necessary groundwork may be sacrificed, and bias and imbalance may creep in. For example, *FOX News* is noted for placing a more conservative perspective in its news analysis. MSNBC could arguably be cited for taking a more liberal perspective in its programming. As a result, you should be cautious when using these sources and make every effort to determine their credibility and balance.

Also the pressure for immediacy in reporting the news, to "beat the competition," can result in inaccurate news. For example, in 2012 the Supreme Court issued its ruling on the Affordable Care Act. According to *CBS News* on June 28, 2012:

> The Supreme Court ruled today to uphold the individual mandate portion of President Obama's Affordable Care Act. All media outlets were sharply focused on the historic decision and attempts to satisfy appetites for instant news brought a string of mistakes in on-air and online reporting.
>
> As the complicated ruling was being announced, CNN reported that the Supreme Court had struck down the individual mandate. The network corrected itself within minutes, but the Internet had already taken note.
>
> Critics were quick to reprimand the cable network.

Television news has a strong visual impact, which can be sensationalistic and diminish credibility. All in all, however, the major networks are considered basically credible, and news programs present the most recent significant research available.

Informational Programming

In addition to news broadcasts there is informational programming. Although it often is filmed or recorded some time before it is shown or aired, informational programming may bring new research to the public for the first time. Viewers can be informed about the latest explorations of the National Geographic Society, or watch the world unfold on TV's Discovery Channel. Sources such as these disseminate a wealth of research information for speeches. Programs aired on the Public Broadcasting System (PBS) particularly strive for independence from outside editorial interference. Generally, informational programming on television has high credibility. As a note of caution—the advent of some "news" programs shouldn't be confused with actual news or credible information and should be considered opinion or entertainment.

One drawback is that this type of programming may lack comprehensiveness. Because the major networks have to provide news in an abbreviated format, stories are not reported indepth. In its favor, television and radio news does continue to cover the same news items for several days, or as long as the story can be updated, building on previous information so the coverage becomes more and more comprehensive.

Unlike news broadcasts, informational programming usually is quite comprehensive. A half-hour show, or even a shorter segment on a program such as TV's *National Geographic Explorer*, provides a wealth of information for the viewer. Because of the popularity of this type of programming, you likely can find written studies to support them using your campus library databases, and your library may have DVD versions of these programs that you may borrow. In addition, these materials may be available via the Internet. Databases such as Lexis-Nexis offer full texts of broadcast news and transcripts.

Interviewing Experts

On a university campus many people can serve as interview resources. College faculty members and administrators, as well as support staff, by necessity must be experts so the institution can meet the needs of its students and other constituents. And college faculty members are specialists in their respective fields. It is only natural that they be called upon from time to time to give information.

In addition, your entire community is brimming with professionals and nonprofessionals who may be able to provide information needed for a speech. Government officials, health-care professionals, librarians, business leaders, individuals who work for nonprofit agencies—all are potential research sources.

Basic Guidelines for Interviewing

Some tips for successful interviewing include:

1. Before asking for an interview you should be familiar enough with your subject to ask enlightened questions. Few experts will be pleased if you schedule an interview and begin with the question, "Would you please explain to me all you know about the problems of rural health care?" This question is so broad that no responsible interviewee would try to answer it—especially for a classroom speech. By acquiring some background information beforehand, you will be able to structure and focus your interview. Other research, including any personal experience with the subject, will give you some idea of how to prepare for the interview.

2. Never simply drop in on someone for a "friendly interview." In the first place, this is discourteous.

Second, an expert needs some time to prepare for an interview. Always arrange in advance for a mutually convenient time to meet, and state clearly the purpose of the interview.

3. Arrive at the interview on time, and be prepared with a complete set of questions to ask. If the person you are interviewing knows you are a student, he or she will likely be more tolerant of your inexperience.

4. Use established questioning techniques. After introducing yourself and reaffirming the purpose of the interview, ask questions that allow the other person to establish personal credibility. For example:

Could you tell me about your role in the research being done by the university that is crucial to climate change research?

This is an **open-ended question**, one that allows the interviewee to select what he or she chooses to include in the answer. In contrast, if you ask, "Are you active in the state's attempt to prevent the expansion of Medicaid?" you may get a one-word answer. Questions should be open-ended because you are trying to elicit a usable response. Yes and no questions do not elicit such responses.

Suppose you are talking to a campus expert who is doing research on alternative energy sources using a specific research procedure. To ask, "Are your research findings generalizable?" probably will insult him or her and also will allow little substance in the answer. Asking instead, "What is the purpose of your research?" will invite the expert to give you an in-depth answer.

In any case, preparing at least some of the interview questions in advance is wise. This will help put you at ease during the interview and show the interviewee that you have come prepared. Once you begin questioning the expert, he or she generally will add information, and the information you gather may suggest new questions as well.

Comparison with Criteria for Good Research

You might ask, "Why bother to interview so-called experts when a trip to the library might provide the same research?" This is a legitimate question. To show how interviews fit into the strategies of good research, let's compare them to the criteria established earlier in this chapter.

First, the interview is *current*. And your speech will gain *credibility*, because the interviewee is an expert and likely will give you up-to-date information. After all, these are the people who constantly are doing research in their field. When interviewing an expert, we are attempting to establish if enough information is available to substantiate our claims. Once an expert has agreed to an interview, you have a great deal of latitude in pursuing the information you need. Those who engage in professional research are thorough within their area of research. It produces *comprehensive* results. And other experts, such as community health and law enforcement personnel, have a wealth of experience to draw from as well.

All things considered, using interviews to gather research support for a speech is a good strategy. Competent interviews are comprehensive and credible, and they meet the criteria of being current. Finally, they allow you to go beyond normal library research and expand your own research capabilities.

Using Library Resources

Your campus library is the outside resource that represents the most extensive source of information to support a speech. A university library holds hundreds of thousands of printed books, magazines, journals, and government publications. In addition, libraries provide access to thousands of digital resources such as subscription databases to help you identify relevant information by subject or topic, digital versions of magazines, scholarly and professional journals, newspapers, government publications, and electronic books. You can locate and view, download, and print full-text resources online via your campus library. Most academic libraries also have an online presence. Among the many topics your library may provide on the Web are resources for conducting research; how to use databases; specific modules or units for various courses, including speech classes; information for conducting research relative to a specific assignment; how to select or look for topics; and how to correctly cite resources using appropriate style citation guidelines.

Digital Resources

The Internet is an excellent source of information for speeches. The three basic criteria for good research—current, credible, comprehensive—apply. For the most part, Internet materials are current.

Mainline sources can be viewed much as a major newspaper can be. And opinion-based materials are identifiable as such, although they may lack credibility.

By becoming more familiar with using the Internet for research purposes, you will be able to more clearly discern what constitutes good research. Like other sources of information, you have to make the ultimate judgment about the currency and credibility of research. Sources such as Wikipedia represent collaborative efforts to provide information about a variety of subjects, but we do not consider sources such as this highly credible because the information they contain is not subject to the traditional scrutiny. Blogs also have become popular, but they can be biased and are not highly credible sources of factual information for research purposes.

As to the third criterion, the Internet can offer fairly comprehensive sources of information. As you discover research online, you will find trails leading to other research sources also available on the Internet. This process is much less time consuming than traditional research and may prove to be more productive in the long run. As one clue leads to another during online research, you may find a wealth of information.

For example, many government documents can be accessed through the Internet. These are considered current, credible, and comprehensive sources of information. Although many students shy away from these resources, students are encouraged to include them in their research. One helpful site is http://www.usa.gov, a federal search tool that gives you access to governmental agencies and congressional records. The U.S. Department of Education website http://www.ed.gov offers a wide variety of information pertaining to many areas of education.

The following criteria are useful for evaluating Internet resources, but they also can be applied to virtually any information resource, including books and periodicals.

▲ ACCURACY

Is the writing style clear and well organized?

Does the information contain any spelling, typographical, or grammatical errors?

Can the factual information be easily verified?

Are charts, graphs, and other visual materials clearly labeled?

Are sources cited?

If sources are cited, are they from reputable publications?

Are statistics used?

If research is presented, is the methodology listed?

Are evaluative reviews available?

▲ AUTHORITY

Who is the author or sponsor?

What are the author's or sponsor's credentials?

What is the author's occupation/profession or sponsor's affiliation?

Is there a way to establish the legitimacy of the author or sponsor? (phone number/postal address)

What is the author's educational background?

If applicable, is the name of the copyright holder given?

Is the source affiliated with a larger, reputable organization?

▲ CURRENCY

When was the piece written?

When was the piece first published or placed on the Internet?

If applicable, when was the piece revised or updated?

If statistics/graphs/charts are used, do they state clearly when the data were gathered and by whom?

If the information is published in different editions, is the edition stated clearly?

Is the time frame appropriate for the information needed?

▲ OBJECTIVITY

Is the information provided as a public service?

Is any bias evident? (e.g., gender or racial bias?)

Is there advertising or sponsorship?

Does the advertising or sponsor have a personal or commercial interest in the issue?

Is the content clearly separated from the advertising?

Is the information intended to inform or to persuade?

👤 SCOPE OR COVERAGE

Toward what type of audience is the information directed?

What is the mission of the document?

Is the information complete?

Has an effort been made to update material?

Using Print Resources from the Library

Despite all the types and sources of research available, many of us still prefer to find information in printed sources. Not all sources of potential information have Web presence. The campus library is your primary repository of printed resources. As you progressed through grade school and high school, you got used to using the library to find books for book reports and then doing term papers requiring multiple sources. This background should be helpful when preparing for a speech. Doing research for a speech and for a term paper is not fundamentally different. In each case you are trying to find materials to support your claims.

Library holdings include serials and periodicals, archival materials that are used to support professional and academic research. The library houses thousands of hardback volumes along with access to an abundance of government documents.

With this treasure trove of information, where do you start? Any in-depth research requires the use of digital information resources such as a library database. Although Google, Yahoo!, and other Internet search engines are popular for general use, they do not provide access to the high-quality scholarly and peer-reviewed information sources that are available only through your library's paid subscription databases. Beginning your research by consulting a librarian is highly recommended. Your campus librarians are information professionals who specialize in providing quality digital and physical sources of information to support the needs of students and faculty members. In addition, librarians can provide you with the skills to be an effective and efficient researcher.

Library Databases

A library database is a large, regularly updated file of online citations, abstracts, and often full-text documents from popular magazines, research journals, newspapers, and other publications. Library databases allow you to search thousands of periodical (magazine, journal, newspaper)

publications at one time through many different strategies.

Using a database, you can search by keyword, topic, or subject. You also can search for resources by a specific author or from a specific publication. Some databases, such as EBSCOhost and ProQuest, are multidisciplinary and cover a broad range of subjects. Other databases are narrow in scope and cover specific subject areas, such as pharmacy, physics, and so on.

Popular Periodicals

We read periodicals casually at home, in reception areas, or in the doctor's office. Periodicals keep us in tune with national or international news, fashion, or sports. These "popular periodicals" are indexed and can be searched using numerous online databases available in your campus library.

Broad, multidisciplinary databases offer excellent coverage of popular periodical literature. In addition to helping you identify relevant articles from hundreds of popular periodicals, these databases provide digital access to thousands of full-text articles. Popular magazines have a number of strengths: They are current and are intended to be briefly informative or persuasive. They provide summaries of research or current findings rather than in-depth information. The information in periodicals is written in a way that is easy for consumers to understand. These articles typically are written by on-staff or freelance writers.

Popular periodicals do have some shortcomings. A major drawback is that they are not as comprehensive as some other sources. An article about texting and driving, for example, might occupy just a single page in some periodicals. One purpose of the newsmagazines is to report new material. Because texting and driving is not a new issue, coverage may be limited.

Research in popular periodicals is still a good strategy because these resources are easily accessible. If you question the comprehensiveness of a source, you can follow up with additional research. Also, the popular resource you are using might suggest additional sources of information. Popular periodicals also are considered credible. This is especially true of newsmagazines. Many of these periodicals now are available online and can be easily accessed from your computer. An excellent source is News Link (http://www.newslink.org), sponsored by the *American Journalism Review*, with links to newspapers, magazines, television/radio stations, and news services worldwide.

Professional Periodicals

We encourage you to go beyond popular periodicals in your research. One area of research often neglected by beginning speakers is found in what we call "professional periodicals"—those that your professors read to stay current in their specific academic disciplines. The field of speech has nearly a dozen such journals, a typical number of periodicals for a given profession.

To determine what journals your library holds, ask the reference librarian for a list, and look up the key words in the topic or subject area. If you fail to find a publication tailored to your subject, search for a publication that reads *Journal of [your topic]*. This might result in your finding a useful publication.

You can be assured that professional periodicals meet the criteria established for good research. The dates on these sources, however, are not the dates of the study of interest; rather, they are the dates when the studies are reported in this periodical. That is not a problem if the research is still the most *current* information available. This is why we recommend using professionally reported studies.

Further, these studies are *credible*. Professional or academic studies are reviewed thoroughly and competently before publication. This is a lengthy process, resulting in a lag time until publication. The thorough review process and the educated readership, however, form the basis for the data's credibility.

The research reported in professional periodicals is *comprehensive*. In these studies a clearly defined research problem is analyzed, and conclusions are drawn. Although the scope of individual research might be narrow, the information reported is comprehensive for that topic.

Clearly, professional and scholarly journals provide much more in-depth coverage of the literature in a specific discipline. The articles are written by professionals/scholars in the field and are intended to be factual and informative and present new research findings. Journals also include a list of references citing the research used in the study. These references can lead to additional sources that may be useful for your research.

Newspapers

Your university or college library will have an extensive collection of major national and perhaps even international newspapers. You might even turn to newspapers as the first source for your research. Some major newspapers, such as the *New York Times, Wall Street Journal, Chicago Tribune,* and *Minneapolis Star and Tribune,* have indexes. Access to these resources is similar to that of the wide array of popular periodicals mentioned previously.

Newspapers meet some of the requirements established for good research but fall short in others. An advantage is that daily newspapers are much more current than popular periodicals. Newsmagazines, for example, are weekly, and some popular periodicals are monthly. For fast-breaking news events, newspapers are a better source of up-to-date news. With the exception of news broadcasts, daily newspapers are the most current sources of information.

Daily newspapers also tend to be credible. Because major national newspapers compete for a national market, overt bias would hurt readership. Newspapers rely in part on nationally syndicated news services. If a publication uses the Associated Press service, for example, its news stories are essentially the same as those of other newspapers that subscribe to the Associated Press. Therefore, national news printed in newspapers is similar, limited only by local editorial decisions. Although these decisions may alter the extent and prominence of coverage, national news coverage in major newspapers using the service is not altered substantially. As with other publications, some bias is to be expected, but this should not hinder your research unless the bias is obvious.

Like popular periodicals, newspapers are not as comprehensive as some other sources. Because newspapers emphasize being current, they often lack comprehensiveness. Newspapers' limited space and their need to cover many news items often mean less coverage of some things. For this reason, you should use additional sources for comprehensive research. By expanding your research base and by using several current and credible sources, you can overcome the shortcomings of newspapers.

Books

Books are last in the discussion of print resources because I believe you should examine other sources of information first—specifically those that are more current. Periodicals meet this criterion, and books often do not. Because writing and publishing books takes longer, books cannot be as current as other sources. An old adage says, "A book is out of date as soon as it is printed." This must be qualified because certain books are ageless. Even so, some books, especially those about evolving technologies, have limited applicability. This does not mean that you should ignore them in your research. It just means that other sources may be better. Finally, the popularity of e-books provides another avenue of access to books.

Summary

The university experience includes research incorporated into term papers and oral presentations. The basic requirements of research are that it is current, credible, and comprehensive. By the time you finish your speech course, you should be familiar with the basic types of research resources discussed here as personal experience and outside resources.

Within this latter classification, *listening/ viewing resources* consist of radio and TV as sources for the most current information. *Interviews with experts* on the chosen topic constitute an excellent source of research. The newest outside resource is the *Internet*, which also may be used to direct you to sources including government documents.

Print resources available in your campus library include popular periodicals, professional periodicals and journals, and newspapers. Finally, library databases will allow you to search thousands of possible topics and subject areas.

Focusing on the Thesis

Suppose you want to give a speech about securing internships during your college or university program. You know that many members of the audience are interested in this opportunity. You may have heard about special programs and websites that provide listings and information about available internships. Your thesis deals with sources of information to locate internships. To research anything about the broader topic of internships would be time consuming and unnecessary. By focusing on the thesis, you constrain your research.

Review Items: Chapter 7

Name _____ Date _____

1. What are the three criteria that good research meets?

    1. _____

    2. _____

    3. _____

2. Explain how listening resources can be used as research.

3. Describe basic interviewing techniques.

4. What are the best print resources to use? Why?

5. Why are popular periodicals used so widely as research resources?

6. How might you evaluate Internet resources for credibility?

7. What function do books have in good research?

8. What use might you make of the reference section in your library?

Supporting Claims and Reasoning

8

The audience may challenge us about where we gained the information we use in our speeches. If we do not have a satisfactory response, our claims may be questioned.

A **claim** is any statement in a speech outline that requires support. The thesis is a claim; main points are claims; and subpoints are claims. The most common way to support claims is through the use of **evidence**. Evidence does not derive from personal experience. Rather, it is directly attributable to outside sources gathered through research, as we learned in Chapter 7.

This chapter explains how to use research-based evidence to support your claims and, specifically, the subpoints in an outline. We will explore various types of evidence. Finally, the chapter covers how to use reasoning to draw conclusions from evidence.

Using Evidence to Support Claims

As a general rule, evidence does not support the thesis or the main points. These are supported by the points immediately subordinate to them. In a normal speech outline, evidence supports the subpoints. During the speech, evidence is introduced orally to

support these subpoints. Evidence is not included in the outline but, rather, is part of the oral analysis presented in the speech. A simple representation of this concept is:

Thesis:

    I. Main point
       A. Subpoint (evidence is used)
       B. Subpoint (evidence is used)

    II. Main point
       A. Subpoint (evidence is used)
       B. Subpoint (evidence is used)

This shows clearly that evidence is introduced orally to support the substructure elements. When those subpoints are supported, the main point is proven. The thesis, in turn, is proven when the main points are supported.

Types of Evidence

In the research you do, you probably will encounter and use three types of evidence: examples, statistics, and testimony. Being able to identify these and knowing how they are used will add to your repertoire of speech strategies.

Examples

We use **examples** in everyday conversation. When we discuss a winning football play or a spectacular musical performance, we are using examples. An example is characterized by the following.

1. An example is a single occurrence of an event.

2. An example depicts something concretely.

3. Alone, an example is not sufficient to prove a claim.

Single occurrences of an event are easy to use as examples. The media constantly present examples of what is good and bad in society. These examples demonstrate something to us.

We encourage you to look for examples because of their concrete nature. People listen to examples. Used properly with other types of evidence, they are part of an effective strategy of support.

An Example of an Example

The increase of diabetes in the United States has reached startling proportions. If you are doing research on diabetes in young children, you may discover many instances of diabetes-related health issues. Suppose your research produces evidence of a young child's death because of diabetes. You can use this single example to support a substructure claim.

Before using this evidence, you must analyze it thoroughly. This analysis is singular; you have one event. You may know that thousands of people are diagnosed with diabetes, but that is not what this example demonstrates. It gives a single occurrence of an event. It shows graphically, or in startling detail, the intensity of an individual fatality of a young child from diabetes. But it does not, in itself, prove the magnitude of the problem. To support the claim effectively, you will have to use other evidence in conjunction with this example.

Statistics

The second major type of evidence you will use, especially in persuasive speeches about policies, is that of **statistics**, consisting of the numbers that compound the examples. Statistics add up the examples and give a total number of specific single occurrences pertinent to the topic being discussed.

In contrast to examples, which are concrete, statistics are abstract. Statistics are numbers, and they can be removed from reality. We may hear the number of deaths from accidental alcohol poisoning each year, yet this number is likely to have little impact on us because it is abstract. More than other types of evidence, statistics depend on your interpretation for clarity and explanation.

Statistics are used in speeches because they show how serious or how widespread a problem is. To be considered seriously, a problem must be significant, or statistically demonstrated.

Notwithstanding the need to use statistics as a major part of your overall support strategy, some cautions are advised.

1. Use statistics sparingly. Audiences are easily overwhelmed by numbers and may not pay close attention to the message.

2. Round off the statistics you are using. If your evidence reports that 29,104 people died as a result of accidental alcohol poisoning last year, it is fair to say that "about 29,000" were killed.

3. Use other forms of support to complement the statistics. Examples are graphic depictions of relevant statistics. Even though a single case may not be sufficient to prove the point, examples are helpful when they accompany statistics.

The use of any type of evidence, including statistics, carries with it an ethical responsibility: The source must be credible and unambiguous.

Testimony

The last major form of evidence you will encounter and use in preparing for speeches is **testimony**. Essentially, testimony is expert opinion and is used widely because we feel a sense of confidence when we are told something by someone we believe is qualified to give an opinion based on his or her background, education, or proven skill. You may have heard someone say, "If so-and-so says it's true, that's good enough for me."

Some key points about testimony are the following:

1. The person giving the testimony must be qualified to render an opinion on the subject. In some cases, the mere mention of the source's name satisfies our curiosity. At other times you must be prepared to give the qualifications of the source.

2. Because he or she is an expert, the source should

be unbiased. All of us, even experts, have biases. Therefore, you should be able to explain why this person is best qualified to give testimony in support of your speech.

3. What appears as testimony also may contain other types of evidence. An expert might give an opinion that contains legitimate statistics or examples, or both. This enhances the testimony.

Testimony is valuable in a speech because, in addition to using an expert, it adds a personal touch to balance the nature of statistics, which are quantitative and impersonal.

In addition to these types of evidence, you might encounter three others when doing research: definitions, illustrations, and analogies. These are not widely used in beginning speeches. In some cases this is because the evidence is quite lengthy, and classroom speeches often have time requirements that make using long pieces of evidence impractical.

▲ **Definitions.** Definitions are of two types. The first is the common type of definition that you would find in a dictionary. If you are doing a speech with major topics or terms that your audience may not understand, you should use (a) *definitions from accepted sources*, and (b) *operational definitions* to lend clarity to the speech. When using an operational definition, you are telling the audience what a term means for the purposes of that specific speech. If your topic is automatic weapons, for instance, you might tell the audience that you are analyzing only weapons that have a fully automatic capability. This constrains your own analysis.

▲ **Illustrations.** Illustrations are extended examples. They are stories. Illustrations are common in long speeches but not in assigned speeches. Because illustrations take a long time to develop, they have limited use in the classroom.

▲ **Analogies.** Analogies are comparisons. They show the audience that something unknown (in your speech) is like something known, so analogies can have a powerful impact. Analogies tend to be long and thus have limited use as evidence in shorter speeches, but they often are used in longer speeches, especially speeches about policies.

All of these types of evidence—those widely used and those less widely used—are part of a strategy that you can use to prove the accuracy of a speech. Evidence supports the subpoint elements,

thereby enhancing the support of main points and the thesis.

If you have good research skills and have thought through how to develop your topic, finding strong evidence will be easy. Your research will yield a large quantity of usable data. Knowing what type of evidence is best to support certain claims will allow you to sift the most advantageous evidence from the research.

Criteria for Use of Evidence

In Chapter 7 we suggested that research should be *current*, *credible*, and *comprehensive*. The same criteria apply to evidence used in a speech.

1. Evidence will have a stronger impact on the audience if it is new, or *current*. If support is current, your claims are more likely to be believed than if they are supported with evidence that is out of date or already known to the audience.

2. Evidence has to be *credible*. In addition to the *source* of the evidence being credible, the *substance* of the evidence has to be credible. When the evidence makes sense, it enhances credibility.

3. Evidence must be *comprehensive*. There must be enough evidence to support the claims you are making. A receiver listening to a single example could conclude that the claim is poorly supported or that there isn't enough evidence to justify the claim. Comprehensive evidence, by contrast, means finding the best evidence and providing widespread proof for that claim.

As you become more proficient at research, you will select better evidence. When you learn what it takes to support your claims, your research efforts will become easier.

Documenting Evidence

Whenever you use evidence in a speech, you must tell the audience where you got it. This is called **documentation**. Documentation is needed to give your claims credibility and to give credit where credit is due. Therefore, when you are doing research and selecting evidence for support, you should write down the following:

▲ Author (one or more persons, an organization, or an agency)

▲ Title of an article in a periodical

👤 Name of the periodical, or title of a book

👤 Date of the publication (and volume/issue, if applicable)

👤 Page(s) on which you found the evidence

👤 Publisher and city (for books)

In some cases the sources of information available will vary slightly, but in most cases your research will yield compatible information about your sources. Whatever the sources of the information, the aim is to let audience members know where you found the material so they will be able to find it themselves if they decide to do so.

Oral documentation in a speech is similar to footnotes or references in a term paper, but oral documentation always appears within the body of the speech. The source of the evidence is named at the point in the speech where it is used. If you restate material from other sources without reference to the subpoint being supported, the evidence may lose its impact. Naming the sources at the point they are introduced also avoids "blanket documentation"— naming your sources at the beginning of the speech and nowhere else. If documentation is given all at once, the audience has no idea which subpoints are being supported.

1. Support necessary claims with documented material.

2. Document all non-original material.

3. Name the source of the evidence before presenting the evidence itself.

4. Use a source reference that is as complete as possible, including title, author, and date of publication.

5. Avoid blanket documentation.

6. When identifying websites, identify them as such, with the title of the web page, site sponsor, and either the date of publication or when you accessed it.

If you listen carefully to professional speakers, such as politicians and ministers, you will notice that they use the credibility of their office to influence audiences, and they also use evidence. When they are using evidence properly, it is documented in some form so you know where they obtained the information.

When citing the source of information, you are explaining to your audience that your claims are supported, in part, by others. You also are giving credit where credit is due—which is necessary when

using anyone's information, whatever the format. Using evidence and documentation should become routine in your speeches.

Following is an example of how to record evidence on note cards for use in a speech.

Recording Evidence for Use in the Speech

Evidence gathered from your research has to be recorded in a form that is usable for preparing the speech and for citing during the speech. We suggest that you record your evidence on 3"×5" or 4"×6" note cards. Below is a sample note card.

> Neporent, L. (January, 11, 2013). Football Head Injuries Increasing Because of Bigger, Faster Players. http://abcnews.go.com/Health/football-head-injuries-increasing-bigger-faster-players/story?id=18183735. Retrieved February 23, 2013, from http://abcnews.go.com/Health/football-head-injuries-increasing-bigger-faster-players/story?id=18183735.

> "It's a condition once known as being 'punch drunk' because it affected boxers who suffered multiple blows to the head, but it is a growing occupational hazard for the hard-hitting sport of football because players are bigger, faster, and more powerful than ever."

This article is about traumatic brain injury in NFL players. The evidence card could carry small notations that will help you in the speech, but we prefer that note cards contain only the complete source information and the actual verbatim evidence to be used in the speech. If you choose not to use a direct quote but to paraphrase instead, the rule still applies.

This note card is to be read in its entirety at the point in the speech when the appropriate subpoint requires support. I emphasize *read*, with the documentation preceding the evidence. You will give the documentation before you read the evidence, so the cards are written that way, with the citation first and the evidence following it. Reading should not stand in the way of strong extemporaneous delivery, but it does lend credibility. After you have selected and recorded your evidence, you have completed a good part of your preparation. As you become a more proficient researcher and speaker, you will find that research strategies and skills in using evidence start to blend.

Reasoning

When each of us woke up this morning, we had to make some choices. For one thing, we had to decide what to wear. That decision might have been influenced by the weather, especially if we have to go from building to building throughout the day. Therefore, before dressing, we often try to assess the weather by looking out the window or by listening to TV or the radio to learn the temperature. This, in essence, is finding evidence. From the evidence we draw conclusions, make inferences, or reason. If we reason properly from our observations about the weather, we dress appropriately. If not, we may become miserable as a result of not dressing properly.

Reasoning is the process of drawing conclusions from evidence. We have learned that evidence comes from outside sources, including examples, statistics, and testimony. From these bits of information, we reason.

Many times we reason instinctively, such as dressing for the weather. In other cases reasoning is more complex. When we know how to reason well, we accomplish two things.

1. We can add reasoning to the wide array of rhetorical strategies available for developing strong speeches. Learning these strategies is a goal of this text.

2. When we know how to reason, we can evaluate more critically the reasoning of others. This, too, is a goal of the course.

The Western world has long treated reasoning as a mathematical equation, asserting that the conclusions drawn from evidence should not vary from person to person. Reasoning, however, is not that simple. Our own values, motives, and experiences influence how we draw conclusions from evidence. Despite these differences, we will analyze the standard ways of drawing conclusions.

General Types of Reasoning

Two of the most widely discussed forms of reasoning are deductive and inductive. These forms have their roots in philosophy.

Deduction

Deduction was discussed by Aristotle and has been accepted as a reasoning pattern throughout the history of rhetoric. By studying deduction, we can see how the basic elements of argument fit together. Deduction reasons from a general statement (about the nature of things) to a specific statement. Students of rhetoric are familiar with the following example of a deductive syllogism:

All men are mortal.

Socrates was a man.

Therefore, Socrates was mortal.

The deductive nature of argument leads us to accept the conclusion as true. In this syllogism we cannot quarrel with the premises or the conclusion. All deductive arguments, no matter how complex, can be illustrated with this pattern. By using the deductive pattern and by placing an individual object in a class of objects, you can attribute characteristics of the class to the individual. But the validity of deductive arguments can be questioned. Arguments can be false, even if the pattern of the argument is accurate. If we accept the pattern and not the substance of the argument, we accept false conclusions, as in the following example:

All students are women.

All women are basketball players.

Therefore, all students are basketball players.

Arguments like this one are considered correct if we adhere solely to the *pattern* of arguments. This argument is patently false, however, if we examine the basis for the conclusion. The pattern shows the conclusion to be accurate, but common sense shows the argument to be invalid.

We often infer that certain things are accurate because individuals belong to a class of objects that have certain characteristics. We can see the danger in reasoning this way. If, however, we can find individual cases that fit a larger general category, and if the argument is otherwise valid, we have developed a strong argument.

Induction

Inductive reasoning works in the opposite way from deductive reasoning. In its most basic form, **induction** examines specific instances of behavior and draws a generalized conclusion. When you use examples as a basis for the conclusion, you are using inductive reasoning. You count the examples and generalize from them. If, for example, you have seven friends who are walking every evening and they all are losing weight, you might reason that they are losing weight because they are getting regular exercise. This is also a causal pattern (which we will discuss later). When using the inductive pattern, you analyze your friends' behaviors (weight loss) simultaneous with walking and conclude that the two are connected.

As with deduction, however, inductive reasoning has pitfalls. Your friends might be watching their diets. They may also participate in other sports or have joined a gym. As with any form of argument, a good public speaker must test the argument for validity.

Specific Types of Reasoning

Deduction and induction are general types of reasoning. They are so pervasive in society that we use them and hear them without much notice. In addition, there are four specific types of reasoning. When you are developing rhetorical strategies for speeches, you will be confronted with choices about how to use evidence. Knowing the specific types of reasoning will improve your ability to draw conclusions from evidence and will help you prepare messages for specific audiences. The specific types of reasoning are generalization, causation, analogy, and authority.

Generalization

When we draw conclusions inductively from evidence (specific examples), we are trying to find a statement that we can apply more generally. We are attempting to make a statement about the nature of things inferred from a few examples or specifics that apply to a whole class of things. When we use **generalization**, we count specific instances and draw a general conclusion from them. The process is similar to induction.

Assume that you are researching a speech on minimum wages. You find one piece of evidence indicating that the majority of people earning minimum wage cannot afford adequate health insurance. You also find evidence that a majority of people earning minimum wage routinely go hungry. Finally, you find evidence that minimum wage earners cannot afford proper housing. You may generalize from the evidence that people earning a minimum wage do not earn enough money to pay for basic needs. If we reach conclusions too quickly from these instances, however, we are developing *hasty generalizations*—faulty patterns of reasoning that lead to erroneous conclusions. For example, let's assume that the test scores from the last speech exam were extremely low. Perhaps your instructor, in an effort to try to understand why the scores were so

low, reasons that the students didn't study enough, studied the wrong material, or didn't take notes during class. The instructor concludes that it is the students' fault for receiving poor grades. Without enough evidence to support these possibilities, the teacher has drawn a hasty generalization.

To avoid hasty generalizations, you must be sure that there is enough evidence to support the conclusion you are drawing. To be effective, reasoning must have **validity**—it must make sense—and that is why you should test the arguments before placing them in a speech.

Causation

A second major type of specific reasoning is **causation**, or **causal reasoning**. When we reason by causation, we are contending that one event or set of events causes another event or events. Some simple examples show how we use causation:

Low attendance in classes leads to poor grades.

Lack of sleep leads to illness.

Drunk drivers kill people.

ACT scores accurately predict college success.

Each of these is an example of causal reasoning. We reason, for example, that a higher ACT score is a strong predictor of success in college. Entrance policies for our universities and colleges are based on this inference, or reasoning. Use of the causal pattern, however, often is erroneous. Even so, it is important, because if you can prove what causes something, you can offer a solution.

To assert that something causes something else is easy. To prove that a causal relationship exists is quite another thing. To test causation, you must establish that the cause actually produces the effect or outcome.

Testing causal reasoning is perhaps more important than analyzing other types of reasoning. Too often we treat the symptoms, or effects, of problems without treating the causes. If causes are established, they can be solved. That is the point of doing **policy analysis**—examining the rules and public legislation that govern our lives. For example, a cause of unemployment is the lack of education. The government could isolate this cause and then develop legislation that can improve educational opportunities.

Causation

The argument is: "The use of salt increases high blood pressure." Conventional wisdom, amply supported by good evidence, proves that the use of salt contributes to an increase in blood pressure. Many other things, however, also contribute to an increase in blood pressure. Thus, the claim is an example of weak causal reasoning. Your family physician would avoid making such a claim until other potential causes had been analyzed. Your role as a policy analyst is similar. You are attempting to discover what causes what.

Analogy

We often argue that what is true for one set of people or institutions is true for another. This is reasoning by analogy. In its most basic form, an **analogy** compares two things, one that is known and one that is not. In this form of reasoning, we apply the characteristics of the known to the unknown. Analogies also can be developed using what has happened in the past as a guide for future planning.

Analogies are tested by examining the situations being compared. If the situations are comparable, asserting that results will be comparable is justified. Because a great deal of argument is based on analogy, testing is important. The first statement in an analogy must be based on evidence that meets all the criteria of strong evidence; the second is the reasoned conclusion drawn from the evidence.

An Analogy

For a long time people argued that the normal highway speed limit of 55 miles per hour should be increased. Proponents of the higher speed limit spoke of "good old days" when the limit was higher. From causal evidence, however, it was concluded that higher speeds contributed to accidents. We used an analogous prior situation and refuted it with causal evidence. Other analogies were used, and eventually it was determined that areas with less traffic had fewer accidents. This led to legislation that allows states to increase speed limits in their states. Throughout the arguments, analogies were developed that related to other times and other places. This was a rather complex argument, complicated by other forms of reasoning. Among them, analogies were used and were tested for validity.

Authority

We also argue from **authority**. We use the expert opinion of others as the basis for our analysis. When testimony is used properly, authority is a basis for our inferences. We reason from the statements of others.

When you develop arguments from authority, the qualifications of the source must be established. This is a good idea when using any type of evidence, and it is especially important when using testimony. It seems to be human nature to question the credibility of another's ideas. If, however, the source of the ideas is established as expert, or informed, we are more likely to believe the expert's testimony. In turn, we are likely to accept the conclusions drawn from the evidence. The reasoning is accepted as valid.

The quickest, simplest test of authority is to examine the qualifications of the source used as an authority. If the source cited is not a true expert, you might well discard his or her conclusions. Speakers have an ethical obligation to establish the strongest basis possible for their arguments. Failing to do so should result in rejecting the conclusions drawn from the evidence. As with any type of reasoning, the argument must be tested.

Another way to test reasoning from authority is to examine the source and the evidence to see if they contain any hidden bias. Most evidence we select strategically for speeches has some bias. After all, we are trying to create the best argument possible. If the bias is blatantly evident, though, the conclusions should be questioned.

Arguing from Authority

In the late 1960s and 1970s many people lobbied for reform of marijuana laws. The political and personal philosophy of those times, coupled with what was believed to be the strongest evidence available on marijuana, led the nation to conclude that some punitive laws were too strict. A major proponent for change was an organization dedicated to the reform of marijuana laws.

In the 1980s the national mood regarding drugs changed, and liberalization of drug laws was no longer widely accepted. During this period the federal Drug Enforcement Agency (DEA) and other governmental groups consistently produced evidence of the harms of marijuana. More recently, many states have changed their laws, legalizing marijuana for either medicinal or recreational use. Many have advocated legalizing marijuana, believing it will reduce some instances of crime and possibly provide a tax revenue source. However, because many governmental agencies are dedicated to the eradication of drugs, for legal and health purposes, its evidence perhaps could be considered biased. Evidence can be strong but biased, and a speaker or analyst of evidence should take this into consideration.

Analyzing Reasoning

As a speaker, or as a critic of the discourse of others, you should be aware that reasoning patterns can be flawed. Knowing the tests of reasoning will help you prepare better arguments and test the reasoning of others. Because reasoning is a process of drawing conclusions from evidence, any form of reasoning you use should be preceded by analysis of that evidence. If the evidence is flawed, the argumentative claim is invalid.

Reasoning often is treated as absolute and unalterable. We reason from evidence and assume that others will reason to a similar conclusion. This process, however, is not absolute. When we reason, we apply our own values, motives, and opinions to the evidence used as a basis for the reasoning. Application of these singularly human concepts can easily alter the outcome of the reasoning.

We realize that the evidence used as a basis for conclusions comes from human sources. Your values and motives will influence how you draw conclusions from that evidence. Your ability to recognize the human element in reasoning will enhance your own analysis.

Summary

Most speakers, both expert and beginner, rely heavily on the analysis of others to support their claims. Use of evidence in speeches is expected of most speakers. As you prepare your own speeches, you can learn by listening carefully to speeches outside the classroom. You will notice that good speakers use strong evidence and give proper credit for it.

The three main types of evidence are examples, statistics, and testimony. In addition, definitions, illustrations, and analogies can be used as evidence. As in research, evidence should be current, credible, and comprehensive. Evidence is documented on note cards, in the order in which it is given in the speech, and verbatim evidence is read from the card for credibility.

To generate credibility, we also use reasoning. We reason, or draw conclusions, about the weather, about the car we want to buy, about the relationships we begin and end. Our inferences are based on observations and evidence.

The general types of reasoning are deductive and inductive. Specific types of reasoning are generalization, causation, analogy, and authority. Awareness of the various types of reasoning will enable you to enhance the pool of available rhetorical strategies as you develop your own public speeches. In addition, knowing how people reason will allow you to better analyze the discourse of others.

Review Items: Chapter 8

Name _____ Date _____

1. What is a claim?

2. What is evidence?

3. How is evidence used to support the structure of a speech?

4. What is documentation, and how is it accomplished?

5. What are examples? How are examples used?

6. What are statistics? How are they used?

7. What is testimony? How is it used?

8. What is definition? How is a definition used?

9. What are illustrations? How are they used?

10. What is an analogy? How are analogies used?

11. What criteria should be applied to evidence before it is used to support a speech?

12. What is reasoning, and what are the two general types of reasoning?

13. What are some specific types of reasoning?

14. How can you test each of these types of reasoning?

Language Style

9

Without shared or mutually understood meaning, even simple words such as *book*, *read*, and *car* literally have no meaning. **Language** is the system of signs and signals that give meaning to communication. How a speaker uses language is referred to as **style**—the choice and arrangement of words that best express the speaker's thoughts. Speaking style involves choices of language usage.

Essential Qualities of Style

Style is situational. A speaker adapts language and modifies language choices depending on the situation. As a speaker, you choose language appropriate for the audience and the communication environment. If, for example, you are to deliver a speech on ethanol to a general audience, your language should be more general and less technical than if your audience is composed of people in the biofuels industry. Many times the situation defines the language choices a speaker makes.

Language style should be individual. As a speaker, you will want to choose words that represent and reflect you. You may have to reword or paraphrase ideas and messages so they accurately reflect you and your personal involvement with your topic.

You also want to generate interest from your audience. This may be accomplished by giving careful consideration to the essential qualities of style: simple, concrete, clear, appropriate, concise, and vivid.

Simple Language

A speech does not have to contain a lot of big, complicated words. You should develop a speaking style that consists of short and easy-to-comprehend words. The simpler the language, the more readily understandable your message will be. If the listeners are forced to stop and think about what some of the words mean, they will concentrate less on the content of the message, which detracts from understanding.

Concrete Language

Concrete means tangible—represented by words such as *car*, *cell phone*, and *textbook*. In contrast are words that are abstract, that is, less easily interpreted, which gives rise to ambiguity in listeners. As a speaker presents ideas during the course of a speech, he or she will have only a brief time to precisely convey messages. Imagine two roommates studying. One roommate, Jason, goes to the refrigerator, and his roommate Dustin says, "Get me a soda, would you?" Jason replies, "Which one?" Dustin then says, "A Coke." If Dustin had simply asked Jason to get him a Coke, his meaning would have been immediately clear. Concrete language is more specific, and abstract language is more general. The following example demonstrates moving from abstract to concrete terminology:

> *Computer*
>
> *Personal Computer*
>
> *Laptop Computer*
>
> *Apple Laptop Computer*
>
> *MacBook Computer*

This example clearly demonstrates the levels of abstractness versus concreteness. The goal of an effective speaker is choosing language that is as concrete and specific as possible.

A related language concern is **slang**. Slang can be either national or regional in nature. During the 1960s, slang included the widespread use of "groovy" and "dig." Today, the phrase "that's cool" may be slang for "great," "fine," "wonderful," or "positive" rather than referring to temperature. "Round file," or "circular file," is sometimes used to describe a garbage can. "Flashback" refers to remembering an event or experience. To "hang it up," means to quit.

When using slang, a speaker must be sure that the audience clearly understands the meaning attached to the words. The language must be appropriate to the audience. This is also true of **jargon**, which is language used by people who work in a particular area or have a common interest (http://www.usingenglish.com/glossary/jargon.html). For example, the phrase "period of economic adjustment" is used to refer to a recession, "reduction in force" means to fire employees, and "paradigm shift" refers to a change in an accepted point of view.

Clear Language

The language in a speech must be instantly recognizable to the audience. Depending on your audience, it may have difficulty comprehending difficult technical terms. If necessary, technical language should be defined in terms that are understandable to the audience. Clear language is free from ambiguity. It consists of words that are common to the speaker and the audience alike.

These common language forms, however, can vary from culture to culture and from region to region.

For example, Kathy Kirk[1] developed a list of examples of regional differences regarding language choice:

Western United States	Eastern United States
submarine sandwich	hero or hoagie
pop	soda
beach	(sea)shore

Assume for a moment that you plan to give a speech on fracking. Before you move into the body of the speech, the term *fracking*—which typically means the process of extracting natural gas from shale rock layers deep within the earth—must be defined and explained.[2]

Appropriate Language

Language must be appropriate for the audience, the situation, and the speaker. It is situational, depending on the audience and the occasion of the speech. Appropriate language depends on variables such as cultural background and demographics. If, for instance, you are discussing with some of your friends the snow removal policy on campus, your language will be informal and appropriate to that level of conversation. But if you are presenting an outline of a plan to the university on ways to improve snow removal policies, your language style will be more formal and persuasive. Your language choice is guided by the situation and the audience receiving the message.

Some language might be considered offensive. Common sense is required. Obscenity and off-color humor are considered inappropriate, as is language that is sexist or racist. Also, you should give special consideration to using the pronouns *he* and *she* when you intend to be inclusive. If you have any doubt about the appropriateness of words or terminology, you would be wise to avoid using them in a speech.

Concise Language

Effective speaking demands that a speaker be as concise as possible. **Conciseness** means using a minimum of words to convey the fullness of the idea. Extra words are distracting. We often use several words when one or two will suffice. A prominent

---

1 Kathy Kirk, *Writing to Standards: Teacher's Resources of Writing Activities for PreK–6* (Thousand Oaks, Calif.: Corwin Press, 2001): 52.

2 http://www.what-is-fracking.com

government official, for example, may respond to an international crisis by saying: "This is a grave and serious matter that we are monitoring closely. Those revolutionary factions responsible will be held accountable for their actions." A more concise format would be: "This is a crisis, and the terrorists will be punished."

Another way to develop conciseness is to avoid redundancy, especially when stringing together adjectives. Examples of redundancy are "an aged, old man" and "a small, tiny particle of sand." Once you get into the habit of cleaning up redundancy, it will seem natural to you. Speaking concisely, however, can be a difficult adjustment. You should allow yourself plenty of preparation time to revise your speech outline and notes, and then rehearse the speech as much as you need to. You may even ask a friend or roommate to listen and monitor the conciseness of your speech. This will improve your speaking skills.

Concise language eliminates verbal clutter. You will become aware of excess verbiage such as "like" and "you know." Many of us use these fillers habitually without realizing it. Breaking yourself of this habit will require effort, but the effort is well worth it.

Vivid Language

During our lifetime we encounter hundreds of speakers and speeches. Most of these speeches and lectures disappear from our memory, but we remember some speeches years later. What made those speakers and speeches so memorable? What did the speakers do to imprint their messages firmly in our minds? Chances are that the speaker used vivid, stirring language to bring the speech to life.

Vivid language is emotive, or emotional, in nature. The speaker uses language that is animated and descriptive, just as a good storyteller uses concrete language that effectively creates a sharp mental image for the listener.

Imagery reinforces the message in the minds of the audience. The more vivid the speech, the more likely it will be remembered. Properly chosen words enable the listener to see, hear, feel, and smell, thereby bringing the speech to life. Following is an example of the vivid language used by Dr. Martin Luther King Jr. in his "I Have a Dream" speech:[3]

---

3 Reprinted by arrangement with The Heirs to the Estate of Martin Luther King Jr., c/o Writers House as agent for the proprietor, New York, N.Y. Copyright 1963 by Dr. Martin Luther King Jr.; copyright renewed 1991 Coretta Scott King. Retrieved from http://www.mlkonline.net/dream.html

One hundred years later, the life of the Negro is still sadly crippled by the manacles of segregation and the chains of discrimination. One hundred years later, the Negro lives on a lonely island of poverty in the midst of a vast ocean of material prosperity. One hundred years later, the Negro is still languishing in the corners of American society and finds himself an exile in his own land. So we have come here today to dramatize an appalling condition.

In a sense we have come to our nation's capital to cash a check. When the architects of our republic wrote the magnificent words of the Constitution and the Declaration of Independence, they were signing a promissory note to which every American was to fall heir. This note was a promise that all men would be guaranteed the inalienable rights of life, liberty, and the pursuit of happiness.

It is obvious today that America has defaulted on this promissory note insofar as her citizens of color are concerned. Instead of honoring this sacred obligation, America has given the Negro people a bad check which has come back marked "insufficient funds." But we refuse to believe that the bank of justice is bankrupt. We refuse to believe that there are insufficient funds in the great vaults of opportunity of this nation. So we have come to cash this check—a check that will give us upon demand the riches of freedom and the security of justice.

This example uses concrete language. It also uses **metaphor**, likening the guaranteed rights of life, liberty, and the pursuit of happiness to a promissory note. The use of metaphor, which compares two totally different things that have something in common, is an effective way to help your audience "see" what you mean.

Vividness also can be created through **simile**. Like metaphor, simile compares different things that have something in common. Similes differ from metaphors, however, in that they may contain the words *like* or *as*. Examples of similes include:

dark as night

quicker than falling asleep

bright as a new penny

clear as mud

light as a feather

Vivid language can make the difference between a dull, lackluster presentation and a speech that is striking and memorable.

Differences Between Spoken and Written Style

Through the years, many studies have been conducted to determine what, if any, differences may be found in the modes by which we communicate. Effective speakers are aware of the differences between oral and written style and adapt their speaking styles accordingly.

One of the primary goals of effective speaking style is **clarity**. This requires that spoken or oral style must be intelligible instantly, whereas written style does not require immediate intelligibility. Because the spoken word is fleeting, the speaker must use words that are clear and understandable. The listener must understand the meaning of each word immediately. By contrast, written style allows the luxury of further explanation, definition, and expansion of words and terminology. Written language can be reviewed and reread so the meaning can be fully absorbed. But as a speaker, you will have to use this one-time opportunity to make yourself understood by ensuring that the language you choose is readily intelligible.

Further, spoken language is more direct than written language. Spoken language is more informal and uses contractions such as don't, can't, wouldn't, and shouldn't. Although informal written language can do the same, the written tradition is generally more formal and avoids those stylistic forms. Spoken language also uses more personal pronouns such as we, our, I, and me.

Spoken style also uses questions more frequently than written language does. Often these questions are rhetorical in nature and do not seek a direct answer from the audience. Stylistically, this is an option, but you should be aware that overuse of rhetorical questions can be distracting.

Imagine that you are listening to a fellow student begin a speech with the rhetorical question, "How many of you work part time or full time?" Your speaker isn't necessarily looking for a show of hands or for an oral response from the audience. By using this rhetorical question, however, the speaker has given you an idea of the topic of the speech and also has linked you as an audience member to the relevance of the topic. As a student, you probably will have a vested interest in the speech.

A successful speaker uses more repetition than a writer does. For example, during his State of the Union address on February 12, 2013, President Obama spoke about gun control legislation in light of a number of tragic mass shootings across the country. As President Obama called on Congress to consider legislation, he reminded his audience of the victims of gun violence, including a young girl from Chicago. With her parents in attendance he said three times, "They deserve a vote." He declared that former Representative Gabrielle Giffords (D-AZ), a victim of gun violence, "Deserves a vote." He talked about the Newtown, Connecticut, shooting massacre by declaring, "They deserve a vote." He mentioned the victims of the Aurora, Colorado, shooting massacre and declared, "They deserve a vote." As the president finished his appeal, he mentioned at least three other shooting events, each time challenging Congress by stating, "They deserve a vote." When the president concluded this section of his speech, the entire well of Congress was on its feet clapping and cheering. This is an outstanding example of the use of repetition to effectively make a point. This section of his speech can be found at: http://www.youtube.com/watch?v=7t_ZygHZZwo.

Another way repetition can be accomplished is through forecasts, previews, and summaries repeating key ideas and main points. Written style uses less repetition. In speaking, however, there is a fine line between effective repetition and redundancy. A simple rule may be: Tell them what you're going to talk about, deliver the message, and remind them what you talked about.

Spoken style also differs from written style in terms of accuracy. By its very nature, spoken style contains more errors and mistakes than written style. Spoken style does not grant the luxury of proofreading and revising. Once the words have been uttered, they cannot be changed. Many of us can think of situations in which we answered a question or responded incorrectly and were forced to live with the embarrassment or verbally correct ourselves. Even so, clarity and precision should be a goal. By selecting language carefully, we can reduce mistakes and misstatements.

Other differences between spoken and written style include the following:

- Spoken style allows more variety and kinds of sentences.
- Spoken style provides more leeway in length of sentences.
- Spoken style uses simple sentences more often.
- Spoken style can include sentence fragments.

- Spoken style uses more monosyllabic than polysyllabic words.

- Spoken style uses more interjections.

- Spoken style uses more indigenous (naturally appearing) language.

- Spoken style has more connotative (emotive) than denotative (detached) language.

Developing Your Own Style

Dynamic and effective speakers have developed a speaking style that sets them apart from other speakers and identifies them as sophisticated, interesting, and enjoyable to listen to. Each of us has the capacity to develop a style that suits our personality and enables us to become effective speakers. Certainly, you are not expected to become the next Martin Luther King, John F. Kennedy, or Maya Angelou. Even so, you can do a number of things to develop a speaking style that uses your skills to best advantage.

1. Analyze your language habits. If you are prone to verbal clutter and need to develop a more concise speaking pattern, work on eliminating these habits.

2. Listen to other speakers and analyze their styles. What language choices do effective speakers make? How could a speaker improve stylistically? What stylistic factors might you avoid? Monitoring the speech and language patterns of people around you will help you develop your own style.

3. Work on correcting mispronunciations. When using words or terminology for the first time or if you are unsure of the proper pronunciation, check the dictionary. Little do speakers realize how adversely their credibility is affected when they mispronounce words.

4. Understand the power of emotive words. They play a critical part in how you are perceived as a speaker. Emotive words can greatly enhance a message, reinforce an idea, and play a crucial role in persuading an audience.

Summary

Language style is an important variable in communication. Many stylistic opportunities are available when developing a public speech.

A good speaking style must create interest. It also should be simple, concrete, clear, appropriate, concise, and vivid. The more you incorporate these essential qualities into your speech, the greater are the chances the audience will pay attention to your communication.

Oral communication has a major drawback: Once spoken, words cannot be taken back. Written communication, by contrast, can be fine-tuned and refined. Also, a speech must be prepared so the audience can quickly absorb it. Finally, good language strategies enhance the listener's retention of oral messages.

Review Items: Chapter 9

Name _____ Date _____

1.   How is language defined in this chapter? How is style defined?

2.   What are the six essential qualities of style? Explain each of them, using an example from your own experiences.

3.   Explain the differences between written and spoken language.

Presenting the Public Speech

10

Thus far we have emphasized content and organizational skills that will enhance your preparation for public speaking. Now we consider the actual presentation, or delivery, of the public speech.

Methods of Delivery

Three principal methods can be used to deliver a speech to an audience: extemporaneous, manuscript, and memorized. Speech professionals in general prefer extemporaneous delivery.

Extemporaneous Delivery

Extemporaneous speaking involves more than the word implies. A speaker using this method of delivering a speech has done a great deal of work to prepare for the presentation. The speaker chooses a topic, structures a thesis sentence with main points and subpoints, completes research, and prepares an introduction and a conclusion. Then the speaker practices many times. Instead of memorization, extemporaneous speaking is based on preparation and practice.

After a speaker has carefully assembled and organized all the information and ideas necessary to construct the speech, the last step is to rehearse it. This enables the speaker to concentrate on delivering the *idea* or *message* rather than the *words*. The speaker should, however, pay close attention to language usage, or style, and carefully select the words necessary to convey the idea. This will ensure language usage that will enhance the delivery of ideas and information.

Reflect on any of the instructors and lecturers to whom you have been exposed. Chances are that they use an extemporaneous style of delivery. They present information and ideas they have delivered many times before. Even though the lectures contain much of the same material, no two lectures are ever the same.

An extemporaneous delivery has a number of advantages.

1. Communicating ideas rather than words diminishes **communication apprehension**. The speaker uses a great deal of energy to deliver ideas rather than expending that energy concentrating on how nervous he or she may feel.

2. Extemporaneous delivery enables the speaker to communicate directly with the audience by establishing direct and sustained eye contact with audience members, because notes are minimal.

3. In extemporaneous delivery the speaker is able to adapt and react to the audience during the course of the speech. The speaker receives a great many nonverbal messages that enable him or her to judge how the message is being received by the audience. Based on this feedback, speakers learn how to adjust the message and delivery. Minimal notes and more eye contact with the audience enable the speaker to evaluate this feedback.

4. Audience members perceive the speaker as conversing *with* them rather than *at* them. This conversational quality is desirable because it sounds spontaneous rather than formal or stiff. Audience members will feel that the speaker is talking to each of them directly.

Manuscript Delivery

At times a speech has to be delivered word for word. If this is the case, **manuscript delivery** may be the most desirable method. The choice to read from a manuscript often is based on time and accuracy factors. Examples are certain political messages and responses from State Department officials.

An obvious advantage of delivering a speech from a manuscript is that the speaker has absolute control over the language, using the exact words desired. The speaker also knows how long the speech will be within a matter of seconds. In addition, the speaker knows what he or she is going to say. Very little is left to chance in terms of content and style.

Manuscript delivery does have a number of disadvantages, though. First, the speaker has difficulty making direct contact with the audience. When he or she is tied to the manuscript, energy is projected downward at the script instead of outward toward the audience. This also means that the speaker cannot readily adapt and respond to the audience. Audience members will not feel that the speaker is communicating with them.

Another drawback of manuscript delivery is that the speech loses a spontaneous and conversational quality. The message may seem uninteresting and even boring. The speaker becomes so busy delivering the words that the message takes a back seat.

A speaker reading from a manuscript should pay close attention to the rate of delivery, emphasis, pause, and stress. This increases the likelihood that the speech will be delivered with energy, spontaneity, and a conversational quality that tells audience members that the message is meant for them.

Memorized Delivery

A **memorized delivery** is from a speech written out in its entirety prior to the presentation and then committed to memory. The manuscript is not used when the speech is delivered.

The speaker who speaks from memory has the opportunity to maintain direct and sustained eye contact with the audience at all times because he or she does not have to look at note cards or a manuscript. The speaker may find it easier to gesture and move around when delivering the speech. In addition, the speaker has time during preparation to control the exact language to be used within the speaking situation.

Offsetting these apparent advantages are some disadvantages. First, memory does not always serve us completely. A speaker who has committed a speech to memory may lose a word in the middle of the presentation. If only a simple word such as *and* or *the* is lost, the entire speech may be gone. Internally, skipping a word triggers panic and may cause the speaker to stumble.

Also, memorized delivery tends to sound stiff and formal. Again, the speaker is concentrating on delivering words rather than the message. In an attempt to remember the speech while speaking, a speaker might stand at the podium with eyes searching for the words. The audience can almost see the teleprompter rolling and, as a result, doesn't hear the conversational quality.

Because the speech is written out beforehand and then committed to memory, the speaker has little room to adapt to the speaking situation and the audience. The speaker doesn't have the opportunity to take advantage of feedback from the audience.

Vocal Characteristics

Most of us take our voice for granted and have little or no idea how it sounds to other people. In reality, the quality of our voice has a great deal to do with how listening audiences perceive us and the message we deliver. Our vocal characteristics are something we can control and even reshape. The three primary characteristics of voice are volume, pitch, and rate.

Volume

Volume is the loudness or softness of your voice. A speaker can use this characteristic strategically to emphasize important elements in a speech. For instance, a speaker can increase the volume to indicate that a certain point is important. A speaker also can indicate the importance of a point by getting softer or quieter, which will cause the audience to have to concentrate even more to hear the point being made. Volume is a relatively simple vocal characteristic for a speaker to utilize.

As a note of caution, your voice sounds louder to *you* than it sounds to the audience. Quite often, beginning students in public speaking believe they are talking at an acceptable level when the audience actually has difficulty hearing them.

The speaker also will have to make adjustments in volume according to the speaking environment. A large room or one with poor acoustics will require more volume, whereas a small room or one with excellent acoustics will carry the speaker's voice adequately. A fundamental way for the speaker to determine his or her volume is to observe nonverbal feedback from the audience. If people are leaning forward, straining to hear, or if they appear restless, this may be an indication to turn up the volume.

Pitch

Pitch refers to how high or low your voice is. When we speak casually or in conversation, we all change our pitch with little or no thought. Public speakers can use this strategy to emphasize certain points and ideas. Variation, or change, in pitch is called **inflection**. A falling or downward inflection is something we do naturally when we finish a sentence or thought. We use an upward inflection when we ask a question or express doubt.

We are all familiar with speakers who fail to use inflection. We say they are speaking in a **monotone**, an expressionless type of delivery that is difficult for a listening audience. A monotonous voice may signal disinterest and a lack of vitality. This quality of voice can be changed and improved upon with practice. You want inflections to happen naturally in your speech. The emotion-laden messages within your speech will give you clues as to where inflections might be appropriate.

Rate

Rate is how fast or slow a person speaks. Usually it is measured in the number of words per minute. The normal speaking range is 90–140 words per minute, although it can range up to 200 words per minute.

When presenting a public speech, the rate of delivery may be either too fast or too slow.

Nervousness often manifests itself in a rapid rate of delivery prompted by a surge of adrenalin. Other speakers deliver speeches at a slow, deliberate pace that may bore the audience. An effective strategy in delivering a speech is to slow down or speed up the flow of words depending on the message. This can be an effective means of making a point or giving prominence to certain ideas.

As to the overall rate of delivery, there is no ideal rate. It varies for each individual. A number of considerations will help the speaker determine the best rate for the public speech. You first should consider the mood you wish to create. Stop and think about the purpose of the speech and the intent. Then give consideration to the listening audience.

The speaker who talks either too rapidly or too slowly may have trouble meeting time requirements, maintaining audience interest, and developing self-confidence in the public-speaking situation. Practicing the speech in advance is important. Noting the rate of speech, the speaker should prepare to meet the required time limit.

Additional Vocal Strategies

Other vocal strategies include projection, pauses, fluent word flow, emphasis and stress, correct pronunciation, and clear articulation.

Projection is different from volume in that the speaker doesn't necessarily become louder but instead gears the energy and message to the audience. Eye contact and voice both focus on the audience. By prolonging syllables and vowel sounds, the speaker also projects the voice outward.

Using **pauses** in a speech can be extremely effective, or it can destroy the message. Pauses are not just mindless periods of silence; they are purposeful, allowing the audience to absorb a point or an idea. Timing is key. For example, a pause should come at the end of a unit of thought, not in the middle.

For beginning speakers, pauses may seem to last a lifetime rather than a few seconds. Therefore, they are tempted to fill the space with sounds such as "ah," "um," or "er." These vocalized pauses can have a disastrous effect on the speech and the speaker. More than one speech class has counted how many of these filler words speakers use in the course of delivery.

Students in a basic speech course have to develop a *fluent and concise word flow*, with a lack of verbal clutter. Practice helps speakers become proficient in the advantageous use of pauses. It enables speakers to make smoother transitions, mentally prepare for the next point of the speech, make physical adjustments at the podium, and allow the audience to solidify an idea.

The use of *emphasis* and *stress* provides the variety and expression that makes listening to a speech a pleasure. These vocal strategies signal the audience the importance of certain points.

Correct *pronunciation* is vital to speakers and their perceived credibility with an audience. Yet, it is amazing how often speakers mispronounce words and key terms. Speakers should check the dictionary for proper or accepted pronunciation of words and terms. The problem is that we usually don't know which words we are mispronouncing. To help remedy this, we might listen more closely to word pronunciations by people who are respected communicators.

Errors in **articulation** differ from errors in pronunciation in that articulation deals with how cleanly and crisply we say the sounds in each word. The cause of misarticulating may be physical, such as a cleft palate, enlarged tongue, missing teeth, or orthodontic appliances. Or it may be a deeply ingrained speaking pattern learned in childhood, such as being encouraged to talk "cute" and say "wabbit" instead of "rabbit," for example.

Some articulation patterns require the help of a speech clinician. Most of us, though, can improve articulation on our own. Americans have a reputation for being sloppy speakers—saying "gonna" for "going to" and "wanna" for "want to," or leaving off the endings of words ("goin" for "going"). In public speaking some speakers mumble and mutter through a speech, perhaps out of apprehension and nervousness. Misarticulating can be self-remedied with some desire and concentrated effort. Speakers should practice saying each phoneme (single unit of sound) crisply and clearly. Improving articulation patterns will enhance your speech delivery skills, as well as the way you present yourself in other social situations.

Nonverbal Strategies

Nonverbal aspects of speech delivery can be just as important as the verbal components, reinforcing messages or contradicting them. A great deal of study has been devoted to the importance of nonverbal communication and its effect on an audience. Some nonverbal elements are eye contact, facial expression, appearance and posture, gesture and movement.

Eye Contact

Eye contact is extremely important. Audiences tend to respond much more favorably to a speaker who is willing to look directly at them when communicating with them. Eye contact should be as direct and sustained as possible, covering the entire audience. For many students in a speech course, the idea of looking directly at the faces of audience members is terrifying. Most of those faces are supportive and friendly, however. In addition, the speaker will be able to evaluate audience feedback and to make adjustments if necessary.

If possible, the speaker should attempt to establish eye contact with the audience 80 percent to 90 percent of the time. Through practice and the judicious use of notes, this is a realistic goal.

Eye Contact

The eyes are a highly expressive feature, capable of conveying many different messages. The eyes can transmit sincerity, hostility, conviction, and warmth, among many other messages. Your eyes must convey messages consistent with the words you say. If you are conveying a happy message, for instance, your eyes must look happy. A contradictory message hampers the speaker's credibility.

Facial Expression

If the eyes can express a great deal, facial expressions are even more revealing. The messages we convey through facial expressions can have more of an impact than the words we say. Think about friends or family members who have assured you that they are doing well when their facial expressions tell you that they are anything but fine. Facial expressions reveal a great deal about our emotional or mental state.

On the one hand, an alert, smiling, and relaxed expression signals a positive attitude to an audience. This invites a favorable response from the listeners. On the other hand, negative facial expressions— scowling, grimacing, and the like—convey insecurity and dissatisfaction with the speaking situation.

The beginning speaker is advised to develop calm and confident facial expressions when rehearsing a speech. Students typically present themselves at the podium with a carefully and meticulously prepared delivery, conveying confidence in their voice but demonstrating pure terror in their facial expression. This inconsistent message may leave the audience unsure about the speaker. Students seem afraid to smile at their audience, but that is exactly what they should do. A smile will put the audience at ease and provide an opportunity for positive feedback from the audience, which will put the speaker at ease and establish a positive communication environment.

Appearance and Posture

Impressions—in particular, first impressions—have a great deal to do with how we are perceived and received. Although you may not be required to adhere to a dress code when presenting speeches in the classroom, personal appearance is an important factor. Appropriate clothing, hairstyle, makeup, and jewelry all say something about our attitudes concerning ourselves, our audience, and the importance of the speaking situation.

We should not go to the extreme of being over-dressed. Flashy or formal clothing draws attention to ourselves rather than the message we are presenting. At the other extreme, blue jeans and shorts are comfortable and perhaps more to our liking, but they may send a signal that our message or the speaking situation is not important to us. In either case, the speaker's credibility may be undermined.

Also, posture says a great deal about the speaker and the message. From the moment a speaker gets up and goes to the podium, the audience starts to develop an impression. Before you open your mouth and *say* something, you convey a message of one type or another. A person who walks straight and confidently to the podium with head held high is communicating nonverbally, "I'm here with a message that I'm eager to deliver. I have confidence in myself and my message."

A straight posture with head up promotes eye contact and conveys a sense of confidence. If using a podium, the speaker should resist the temptation to "rest" or lean over. Perhaps it will be easier to maintain better posture by standing away from the podium, holding any notes at a comfortable level with elbows at waist level.

After delivering a speech, the speaker should resist the temptation to race back to the safety of a seat. Many fine speeches have been destroyed by a hasty exit. When walking back to your seat, take your time, hold your head up, and keep your shoulders back.

Gestures and Movement

Gestures and movements have to do with how speakers use their bodies to create a total message. Gestures deal specifically with the hands, arms, and shoulders. Effective use of gestures reinforces a message, providing emphasis. Gestures should be natural, not forced. Imagine a speaker who forces a sweeping, stiff-arm swing to dramatize a point. The impression is just the opposite, detracting from the message.

For many of us, gestures happen naturally. We find it nearly impossible to speak without using our hands and arms. If this is the case, we should consider a couple of things. First, the gestures should not be so distracting or numerous as to take away from what we are saying. Gestures also should be within the audience's field of vision. This means that gestures should be above the waist but not so high as to raise the arms. Outward movement toward the audience also is desirable. When using gestures timing is important, because the intent is to highlight and reinforce an idea. Poorly timed gestures undermine the message and distract audience attention.

To determine whether gestures are appropriate, first ask yourself: "Is this natural for me? Do I appear awkward or uncomfortable?" Second, consider your audience. Are the audience members young and energetic? Is the audience a group of professionals? Is the audience a group of elderly citizens? The answers to these questions will give you a clue as to how to use gestures in the speech. Finally, consider the speaking situation. Is the setting a professional convention, a "roast" held in honor of a club member, a memorial service? As a simple rule, the more formal and serious the occasion, the fewer gestures should be used.

Physical movement may play an important role in maintaining and regaining audience attention. It seems unnatural for a speaker to stay fixed in one spot for the duration of a speech. For movement to gain positive attention, it must be purposeful. Speakers who pace back and forth, shift their weight from foot to foot, rock back and forth, put their hands in and out of their pockets, tap on the podium, fidget with note cards, or nervously tug on clothing are using movement to their disadvantage.

Many of these movements are a product of nerves and apprehension. In any case, they are distracting and interfere with communication.

Speakers can make optimum use of movement with timing and planning. Taking a couple of steps when making a transition from one idea to another can be effective. Speakers should read audience feedback. If you sense that the audience is becoming restless, take a few steps forward to lessen their listening fatigue. Again, this movement must be natural and within the audience's field of vision. Speakers should practice movement within the presentation of the speech, work with the note cards, and make use of key transitions to maintain audience interest.

Summary

A well-organized and researched speech will fall on deaf ears if it is not delivered effectively and energetically. Therefore, the public speaker must develop delivery skills. A strong delivery ensures that the ideas and message are communicated clearly, free of distraction.

The three basic methods of delivery for a public speech are extemporaneous, manuscript, and memorized delivery. The preferred method of delivery for most speaking situations is the extemporaneous method. This style uses minimal speaker notes and is based on rehearsal and practice. It focuses on delivering the idea or thought.

Particular attention should be paid to the speaker's voice, including the characteristics of appropriate volume, pitch, and rate of delivery. Additional voice strategies include adequate projection; well-timed use of pauses; proper pronunciation; and clean, clear articulation.

Important nonverbal delivery strategies include direct and sustained eye contact, consistent and appropriate facial expressions, and well-timed gestures and physical movement at the podium. A speaker's polished personal appearance and good posture round out the positive picture.

Allowing adequate time to practice all aspects of the delivery process will ensure a well-rounded presentation. Using good delivery strategies will produce a positive experience for the speaker and audience alike.

Review Items: Chapter 10

Name _____ Date _____

1. What is extemporaneous delivery?

2. What is manuscript delivery?

3. What is memorized delivery?

4. What are the advantages and disadvantages of each type of delivery?

5. What are the major vocal characteristics?

6. What are some nonverbal characteristics, and how can they be used in public speaking?

Informative Speaking

11

In this era of rapidly increasing information, we must rely on fellow human beings more than ever to exchange knowledge. For this to happen, information must be conveyed and received accurately and precisely. Examples of information sharing include providing directions to a building on campus, explaining the different types of social media, describing climate change, and explaining cybercrimes. In each of these examples the need for clarity of information is obvious.

Your role as a student/citizen/analyst necessitates skill in information sharing. For that reason, **informative speaking** is a fundamental part of your education. As a college student you are exposed to informative speaking in the classroom. The business and professional world revolves around informative speaking. As a citizen of the global community, much of what we learn and understand about our world comes through the informative speaking process.

Features of the Informative Speech

Informative speaking has one primary goal: to relate information and ideas. Persuasion is not a goal of informative speaking, because the speech to inform does not ask for change or action from the audience. The informative speaker sets out to present information that is unfamiliar to the audience or to expand on knowledge the audience already possesses. The speaker wants nothing from the audience except attention and willingness to listen.

A common error in the informative speech is that speakers take a persuasive posture with a topic without realizing it. An example of an appropriate thesis statement for an informative speech on the topic of early childhood education programs is:

Early childhood education programs provide a variety of opportunities and experiences for young children.

A thesis statement on this same topic, but with a persuasive approach, is:

The U.S. Government should fund early childhood education programs.

Although both thesis statements deal with the same topic, the intent of each is totally different. When developing a topic for informative speaking, speakers have to remember that the purpose of the assignment is to *inform*.

Clarity

An essential element in a speech to inform is **clarity**. If informative speakers want to be readily understood, the topic must be clear to the speakers themselves. If the topic is unclear to them, they must ask themselves how clearly this topic can be developed and conveyed to a listening audience.

Developing clarity with a topic involves a number of considerations.

1. If the topic is technical in nature, you will have to develop the topic in a manner that a layperson can easily understand.

2. If the topic under consideration is too broad, you may have to narrow it.

3. You may have to define terms and explain ambiguous language.

4. You should have a well-worded thesis statement and identifiable main points.

You can achieve clarity by choosing your words carefully and organizing your ideas well.

Understanding

When we speak of understanding, we may be

1. relating information that is unfamiliar to the audience, or

2. expanding on information the audience already knows.

Consider the topic of corn, for example. The audience probably knows about corn production in the United States, and that corn has many different uses in food production as well as in the production of ethanol. The audience may not know, however, that corn is used to manufacture many different products besides food and fuel. They are familiar with the topic, but their present knowledge can be further developed.

Analysis

Informative speaking requires that the speaker thoroughly develop the topic under consideration. Because of restraints on time and the assignment, a speaker may benefit from narrowing the topic further to allow for more detailed examination and in-depth analysis. In contrast to persuasive speaking, which takes a more biased, one-sided approach to a topic, the informative speaker must present all ideas and information available on a topic, providing an impartial, unbiased presentation.

Guidelines for Informative Speaking

When developing an informative speech, the speaker must use all of the skills discussed in the previous chapters. In addition, the following suggestions are useful to informative speakers.

Selecting a Topic

When choosing a topic for informative speaking, look for a subject that lends itself readily to the informative speech. Topics that are poor choices for the informative assignment include those dealing with personal values and beliefs. Many topics that are controversial or are matters of policy also may be poor choices for an informative speech because they can easily evolve into persuasion.

Topics should not be chosen hastily. A topic may be too broad or too difficult to analyze. A hastily chosen topic may be difficult to research. Choosing a topic because your roommate or friend has used it, or because the assignment is due and you have procrastinated, can have disappointing results.

Selecting a topic for an informative speech also depends on your audience. When looking for an audience-centered topic for the informative speech, you should consider the audience's background. Do its members have knowledge based on firsthand experience or casual knowledge based on reading or exposure to the media? Reaching the audience is much easier when the members can relate your ideas to their own experiences. For instance, a speech on the different kinds of cocurricular activities available to college students will capture their attention and be easily understood by a college class.

Topics must be developed in a way that is appropriate for the audience. A speech describing the process of developing and designing cars will be approached in a more technical manner if the audience is composed of engineers rather than of college students with no background in engineering.

A speaker should talk with authority and competency. Therefore, you should speak on a topic that you understand and about which you are well informed. Your role as an informative speaker is to provide your audience with information that is new to them. Listeners have to believe that listening to what the speaker has to say is in their best interest. If you choose a topic that you know well and develop a clear, understandable message, your audience will benefit.

An Appropriate Topic?

Imagine the difficulty that a representative from the Department of Health and Human Services might face when addressing community and campus leaders about the problems of individuals who literally cannot afford to buy food. This audience likely has a better understanding of the number of citizens and students in the community who are struggling to afford food, and they also have a better understanding of the services available in the community. Unless the representative has done extensive research and worked with community and campus leaders to appreciate the precise extent of the problem and what measures are in place to assist people, this would be an inappropriate topic for the speaker and the audience.

Assessing Audience Knowledge

A student delivered an informative speech about sinkholes. The student explained that sinkholes are commonly found in karst landscapes. What the student failed to do was define "karst landscape." As a result, the audience was left wondering what the speech was about.

A common error in public speaking is to assume that audience members already know more than they actually do. As an informative speaker, you might assume that you are providing information based on what your audience already knows, but novice speakers tend to overestimate what the audience knows. Therefore, an informative speaker should take great pains to explain, define, and clarify any terms, concepts, or ideas that may interfere with understanding the message. Successful speakers approach a speech as if the audience is hearing about the topic for the first time, thereby reducing the risk of being misunderstood.

Using Nontechnical Topics and Language

Informative speeches for a general audience must be developed on the presumption that the audience has limited or no background in the subject matter. Topics laden with technical terms and topics dealing with technical processes or concepts are difficult to explain to a general audience. Audience members have varying capacities to understand technical concepts in keeping with their background and exposure to the material. What may be understandable to you might be highly technical and meaningless to others.

Since the advent of alternative energy resources, many students have used this topic for informative speeches. Unfortunately, speakers often try to explain in scientific or technical language how solar or wind energy works. Unless the audience has the relevant technical background, it is difficult to present a clear and thorough explanation. Many terms have to be defined, and the needed scientific knowledge requires explanation before most people can understand them. The assignment and audience may not allow enough time and shared knowledge between speaker and audience to create a successful informative speech.

Topics do not have to be technical in nature to use highly technical terminology. All subject areas use language that is specific to them. For example, the topic of federal government budgets is complex. Terminology associated with federal budgets includes debt ceiling, sequestration, and national debt. A federal lawmaker or economist will easily understand these terms. The layperson, however, may not thoroughly understand this **jargon**. The public speaker must strive to adapt language of a technical nature to the general audience and to define the terms used.

Adapting the Topic to the Audience

A common concern of students in a public speaking course is whether class members will be interested in the topics they choose for their speeches. What is interesting to one person may be of little or no interest to another. If you have settled on a topic you like and find interesting, you have completed the first step in developing a speech that your audience also may find interesting. Next, a successful speaker should take steps to adapt the speech to the audience, letting audience members know that the speech offers something for them and that this information is important.

A speech on the topic of sleep deprivation was developed in a way that involved the audience and aroused interest in listeners who initially were somewhat uninterested in the subject. The speaker began his speech this way:

> *As the semester wears on, do you find yourself tired, lacking energy, unable to focus, and cranky? You may even find that you are catching every cold, feeling sick, and even depressed! You may be interested to know that one of the contributing factors to these symptoms is that you are not getting enough sleep. Knowing the effects of sleep deprivation can help you to start changing your routine and eliminating these problems.*

This speaker makes reference to an activity common to all audience members: sleep! His references to college students' need for the information in the forthcoming speech and its value have a positive effect on the audience.

In the course of the speech, the speaker adapted the main points to the audience. The first point elaborated on the importance of sleep. The speaker pointed out that most college students do not get enough sleep. The second point informed the audience that there are a number of simple things that can be done to ensure they are getting enough rest. The final point of the speech explained that there are resources available to assist students in getting the sleep they need. The speaker used evidence based on research to develop the speech and support the points being made. By adapting this information to the audience, the facts took on more significance.

Types of Informative Speeches

Topics that may be chosen for informative speeches cover a broad spectrum. Therefore, classifying potential topics by categories is helpful. This aids the speaker in identifying how best to approach the topic and also may give clues to organizational patterns.

Explanation of a Process

A process topic can be an interesting and suitable choice for an informative speech. Topics may range in complexity from heart bypass surgery to explaining how to bake bread. **Process speeches** explain in step-by-step detail how something is done or how something is made. When organizing a process speech, you begin with the first step of the process and follow through to completion. A chronological organization pattern often works well for this type of speech.

Time restraints, however, may prohibit using chronological organization because this form tends to take more time than may be allowed, particularly for complicated processes such as preparing for a marathon. And it may lose the audience's interest in the details. As a result, if you are giving a speech on a process, you should include the major points only in the outline, but the structure will lend itself to stronger analysis when delivering the speech.

Examples of speeches on understanding a process and performing a process are as follows:

Understanding a Process	*Performing a Process*
making stained glass	windsurfing
pharmaceutical compounding	raised-bed gardening
wind turbine production	setting up a Facebook page
ice cream production	training service dogs

Description of a Person

Many of us have been required to do a report on a significant person—maybe when we were in elementary school, or perhaps for a club project. Whatever the occasion, describing a person and his or her impact on the world is something with which we are familiar. People make fascinating subjects for research and study. Thus, choosing a person for an informative speech can be a wise decision.

When speaking about a person, a number of factors should be considered. Selecting a person who is relatively contemporary may be a good idea. Although history is replete with interesting people, the audience might identify more with your speech if you are dealing with a living person.

Second, you should structure your speech around the person's significant contributions or unusual attributes. You do not want to develop a biography about the person. Few people will be interested in a chronological history of or a professional list of films that George Clooney has starred in, for example. However, his humanitarian work finding a resolution for the Darfur conflict, his fund-raising efforts for the 2010 Haiti earthquake, 2004 Tsunami, and 9/11 victims, and creating documentaries to raise awareness about international crises would make an interesting informative speech. The following is a sampling of the many different possibilities for people who have influenced society:

Mark Zuckerberg	Sir Richard Branson
Ang Lee	Melinda Gates
Lady Gaga	Michael Bloomberg
Jeremy Lin	Aung San Suu Kyi
Nate Silver	Queen Rania of Jordan

Description of an Animal

People in general are fascinated by animals, and many of us have pets. The diversity of the animal kingdom provides a wide range of species to explore. The choice of animals as a topic for an informative speech is well suited to many speakers. Topics may range from common household pets, breeds, exotic and endangered species to unusual habits and characteristics of certain animals.

When developing an informative speech about an animal, speakers should look for unique features that make the animal or species distinct. Giving information about an animal that is not known universally will interest an audience and provide valuable learning. Below are just a few ideas borrowed from the animal kingdom:

olm	elephant bird of Madagascar
vampire squid	pangolin
baton blue butterfly	Angora rabbit
moon jelly	portia spider

Description of a Place

For many, traveling to faraway places is only wishful thinking. Some of you may have had the opportunity to make this wish a reality. If so, describing a place is a natural choice for an informative speech. But the choice of places is not limited to well-known countries such as England or Mexico or states such as California or Alaska. This category covers much more. Perhaps you have vacationed in the Gulf of Mexico, toured Yosemite National Park, or studied abroad in Turkey. Interesting and historical places may be found in your own community or hometown. Many students have used this category for informative speeches and are surprised to discover the wealth of information it contains. Examples of places include:

Arlington National Cemetery

Great Barrier Reef

Golden Temple, India

Petra, Jordan

Canadian Rockies

Description of an Object

Descriptions of objects have limitless potential for an informative speech. Speeches that describe objects can be organized in different ways—spatially, topically, or chronologically. When speaking about an object, you may have to limit the topic of your speech to a specific aspect of the object. For example, a speech describing smartphones may have to be limited to the various capabilities of the phone, as opposed to describing all of the different popular applications available. Other sample topics are:

fortune-telling teacups	insulin
Bedouin clothing	solar panels
iPad	the Hope Diamond
Blu-ray discs	the corpse flower

Description of a Structure

Many naturally occurring and man-made structures are suitable topics for informative speeches. Structures differ from objects in that they are not easily moved and may be difficult to touch or hold. Quite often a speech about a structure is organized spatially as the speaker describes the main features of the structure. A prominent example is Stonehenge. In this type of speech, the number of megaliths, the circular arrangement of the structure, and the nearby earthen embankments could be described.

When presenting a speech that describes a structure, you are attempting to produce a mental image in the minds of your listeners. Thus, you will want to create a vivid picture. The following list represents a few possible topics for the informative speech describing various structures:

the Alamo	Buckingham Palace
Lighthouse at Alexandria	Channel Tunnel
Brooklyn Bridge	Lincoln Memorial

Description of an Event

Each of us has experienced significant events that have influenced who we are. The world around us is shaped by events that happen every day. Some of these events touch our lives directly, and others have less direct impact. They often become milestones when we remember where we were or what we were doing when something happened. The choice of events as a category for informative speeches offers a unique approach. You have the luxury of hindsight to describe the impact and influence that events have had in shaping your history, your country, and your world.

Historical events offer a great many possibilities for informative speeches. American history is littered with assassinations and deaths caused by guns. Abraham Lincoln and John F. Kennedy were both assassinated while serving as president. President Ronald Reagan was a victim of an assassination attempt. In recent history, we have witnessed multiple mass shootings involving a sitting U.S. representative and hundreds of victims in malls, movie theaters, and schools. Gun violence affects how we view society and how Americans are perceived by others throughout the world. The creation of the cable news channel, CNN, changed the nature of news reporting, allowing 24/7 access to breaking news and information. When Facebook was launched in 2004, it revolutionized the concept of social media and the way we communicate and interact with the world. These are all examples of events that have had a social, political, moral, or economic impact on our lives.

Certainly, many other events have affected our lives as well. These events offer the opportunity to learn more about our world. Examples are:

presidential inaugurations

Sturgis Motorcycle Rally

Chinese New Year

Super Bowl

9/11 attack

Explanation of a Concept

Concepts are ideas, values, and beliefs. They are more abstract and complex than objects or events and, as a result, can be much more difficult to explain, especially if the audience is hearing about the concept for the first time. The speaker must clearly define the concept early in the speech. Using comparisons and examples helps illustrate the concept and ensure that the audience understands it.

We deal with concepts every day, but we do not all attach the same meaning to a concept. We all interpret things differently. For instance, the concept

of goodness carries a different meaning for each person. For some people, goodness may manifest itself as in service to others, while for others it may mean holding the door for another person or remembering friends on their birthdays. Other examples of concepts are:

austerity	vegetarianism
lifelong learning	liberalism
justice	faith

In all of the above categories, students can find a significant number of topics that stimulate their thinking. Informative speech topics are limitless. The creative speaker uses public speaking strategies to develop an interesting message for the audience.

Summary

Informative speaking is prevalent in contemporary life. Business and professional institutions require effective speakers to convey vast amounts of information. We use this information as a basis for decision making. Developing skill as an informative speaker requires practice and work.

The goal of informative speaking is to convey a clear message. Transmitting information and relating ideas to an audience requires clarity of language and careful organization. Attention to factors such as topic selection, audience background, and technical language enables speakers to develop interesting, comprehensible, and enjoyable informative speeches.

Public speaking strategies must be analyzed carefully to allow the best choices for a given audience. Close attention to evidence and analysis of the factual material is necessary. An informative speech should be organized to have the maximum impact on an audience. Proper, vigorous delivery will enhance the entire message.

Topical categories for informative speeches include processes, persons, animals, places, objects, structures, events, and concepts. Informative speaking is a logical prelude to persuasive speaking, the topic of Chapter 12.

Review Items: Chapter 11

Name _____ Date _____

1. What is the primary goal of informative speaking?

2. What are the major features of an informative speech?

3. Explain how to choose an informative topic that is relevant to the audience.

4. Explain the categories of informative speeches described in the chapter.

5. Which organizational patterns might be best suited for each of these speeches?

Persuasive Speaking

12

Every day we use persuasion in our family relationships, our careers, and our casual encounters. Persuasion may be minor, such as persuading a friend to do something; or it may be important, like persuading a friend not to drive when he or she has had too much to drink.

Persuasive speaking has certain characteristics in common with informative speaking. You are expected to use research that meets the criteria established in Chapter 7. Then you select the best evidence from that research, keeping in mind that evidence also must meet certain criteria. You are expected to find an organizational pattern that best allows you to persuade. Your language usage must be appropriate to persuasion. Clearly, persuasive speaking is much like other speeches.

In other ways, though, persuasion is not like other speeches. Persuasive speaking carries with it more power than informative speaking. If, in an informative speech, you are discussing the dangers of too much salt in our diet, you do not expect to influence audience members. The audience listens, perhaps retains the information, and may be better

for it. If, however, you show a specific harm to the health of individuals who consume processed foods containing salt and then, as a persuasive goal, ask your audience to do something, your message is more likely to have an impact on the audience. Even though the strategies are often the same, persuasive speaking has greater outcomes.

Persuasive speaking usually falls into three categories.

1. Trying to persuade people that something is *factual* (this is different from an informative speech).

2. Attempting to convince people that something is *valuable*.

3. Trying to persuade someone to adopt a certain *policy*.

Each of these also has a negative side—that something is not factual, is not valuable, or should not be adopted. Most speech texts treat these components as analysis (and persuasion) about questions of fact, questions of value, and questions of policy.

Questions of Fact

Analysis of a question of fact brings you close to giving a simple informative speech. To show what we mean, let's consider a few questions of fact:

- Should there be a playoff system for NCAA football?

- Should the United States limit the amount of foreign aid it pays?

- Can diet alone reduce blood sugar?

- Should the United States reform criminal sentencing laws?

When delivering a speech on a question of fact, the speaker attempts to answer the question for the audience. The answer is not a simple yes or no, however. Nor is the speech simply an informative one, because you intend the answer to have a persuasive impact on the audience. In the above examples, you may want the audience to believe that a playoff system is necessary. You want the audience to be influenced about the amount of foreign aid the United States should provide. You want to persuade audience members to carefully monitor their diet to reduce blood sugars. And you want the audience to do something about sentencing guidelines. Essentially, you are an advocate for the answer, and you provide a biased answer.

The thesis sentence in speeches on questions of fact answers the question of fact. A thesis sentence for the foreign aid question above may be:

The United States government provides billions of dollars in foreign aid, while our economy is struggling at home.

This is not an informative sentence about foreign aid; it is a sentence about the amount of foreign aid and how it is adversely affecting our domestic economy. As an advocate, you are in favor of reducing foreign aid.

Beyond the thesis sentence, the speech structure develops normally. The organizational patterns introduced in Chapter 6 provide a selection of strategies to use for organizing the body of the speech. The above thesis suggests a topical pattern. The main points could be phrased:

I. Limiting the amount of foreign aid will help to reduce our national debt.

II. Limiting the amount of foreign aid will free up funds for domestic programs.

This may seem like a simple way to structure the body of a persuasive speech—and it is. Yet it is sufficient to establish the accuracy of the thesis, and that is the point of the speech.

The next step is to establish the accuracy of each main point by supporting it properly with substructure elements. These, in turn, have to be supported with evidence. When the speech is put together, it should be phrased in persuasive language and delivered positively.

Most of the preparation for a persuasive speech is similar to the preparation for an informative speech. Both cases require strategic choices about structure, language, evidence, and delivery. In the topic developed above, the purpose of the speech differs, and, therefore, some of your choices will differ. Choosing persuasive tactics that will move the audience is part of using your audience analysis skills.

Questions of Value

We all hold values of some type. We base our judgments about right or wrong and good or bad on these values. We often wish to communicate these values to others, and we do so by analyzing questions of value. We take a stand on something based on our perception of its value, and we communicate that stand to others. Again, we can look at some examples.

Most of us, for example, have some appreciation for small businesses. We shop at small, family-owned businesses; family members may have their own business; or we know people who own small businesses. You might believe that taxes on small businesses are too high and, as a result, you see that it is difficult for small-business owners to stay in business. You may want to persuade your audience that the government needs to provide more incentives for small-business owners through reduced taxes and initiatives to help them expand. Clearly, you value the role of small business in our communities and in our economy. You might develop this into a speech on the subject by asking the question:

What responsibilities does the government have to help support small-business owners?

Your answer is aimed at persuading the audience. This is the intent of the speech. The process you follow is similar to that outlined above: Develop a thesis, a support structure, and evidence; phrase the speech persuasively; and deliver the speech.

In a broad sense, questions of value are about concepts, including religion, politics, societal views, human rights, and government rights. People believe that their right to freedom of speech should be protected. We hear that illegal immigrants have certain rights while being detained. We also hear that our country has certain responsibilities regarding processing illegal immigrants. These are all value positions. A politician arguing that all American citizens have to complete a year of community service (without providing further detail) is setting forth a value in a persuasive format. A policy speech on the same subject (which we will discuss next) goes far beyond the value speech in terms of detail.

Fact and value questions often are used explicitly or implicitly as the basis for policy speeches. An examination of the subjects above will suggest policy options.

Questions of Policy

Governments and various agencies place limitations on our day-to-day lives. These agencies make policies that influence us. Because policy analysis is so important in our society, we will devote most of this chapter to it.

If you listen to the nightly news or check online news sites, you will find topics pertinent to public policy. These topics might include:

medical marijuana	cyberbullying
voter registration	gun regulation
civil unions	health insurance
security screening at airports	steroid testing in professional sports
renewable energy	Social Security
climate change	hate crimes

The list can go on, limited only by a policy issue that is important to you. As with any topic, you should select one with which you are comfortable.

From this topic you can phrase a question of policy and ultimately develop a thesis. A general question of policy might be phrased: "What should the United States do about _____?" This question will guide your research, and eventually your speech will take form.

Phrasing the Thesis

The thesis for a policy speech answers the question in a general way. To be complete, the thesis in a proposition of policy must advocate a change in a present policy. The speaker seeks to change the status quo. The thesis, too, must be enforceable. This means that it must have a reasonable chance of implementation through a more detailed policy. For example, banning guns entirely is not likely to be successful, whereas stricter control of various weapons may be successful.

You don't have to consider an entire policy. You might decide to examine a small portion of a larger policy. If, for instance, you are concerned about renewable energy, you may decide to concentrate on wind energy. This is a much more manageable topic for a classroom speech than addressing the wider topic. As with any topic, narrowing it to a reasonable point is important, and the thesis can help you do that.

Most policies are supported by enforcement mechanisms; penalties are imposed for not following policies. You are exposed to these policies in your university, in the legal system of your community, and in federal and state laws. That is why we encourage a thorough analysis of enforcement as a part of the preliminary work you will be doing to prepare a thesis.

From another perspective, a thesis sentence contains

1. an *agency* that has the power to act in the matter you are considering,

2. a *mandating word* such as *should*, and

3. an *action* that the *agency* should take, phrased in general terms.

Policy speeches need not deal only with governmental policy. Many policies are not the province of local, state, national, or international governments. Yet they, too, are valid concerns for policy discussions. If you are interested in quasi-public policies, you should explore them.

A Quasi-Public Policy

The university setting allows ample access to athletics in many forms. The rules or policies that govern collegiate athletics are, in a way, public rules. They are in the public eye. In many cases the National Collegiate Athletic Association (NCAA) proposes and enforces regulations for college athletes. Do you agree with all of these regulations?

As with any speech, phrasing the thesis is important. It gives you focus for research and a clear object of proof.

Preparing the Body of the Policy Speech

A complete policy speech has four elements, each of which can be a main point for the speech: the problem, the cause, a plan, and justification. Each element is important because, taken together, they allow for a workable solution for the problems discovered through research and explained in the body of the speech.

The Problem

The problem may be stated as the harm in a present policy, or an **indictment.** An indictment is a charge against society, a statement that something is wrong. In this sense, an indictment is analogous to a legal indictment, in which a charge is handed down against an individual for an alleged criminal offense. We often read or hear of a person being indicted for fraud, murder, or other crimes. An indictment for a policy speech is much the same. After strong research, you are able to "file charges" against a part of society represented by policy.

A policy analogy for the indictment can be found in the health-care field. Indictments are symptoms indicating something is wrong in society. You are doing a diagnosis of society, much as your family physician performs a diagnosis on you. He or she first looks for symptoms of a problem—weight gain, loss of appetite, fatigue, and so on. From these, the physician begins to look for causes of the symptoms.

To determine an indictment against society, you likewise ask: "What is wrong?" Your answer becomes the indictment. We will show a complete outline later, but for now you should know that the harms, or indictments, become part of the main point structure of the speech.

Developing indictments is important because these are what make people take notice. Outward signs of problems attract attention.

The Cause

Most of us play amateur physician at times. We identify symptoms of our illnesses. Many of us have seen evidence of a crime—someone running a stop sign, underage consumption of alcohol, or someone cheating in class. Thus, in everyday life we identify what's wrong. To solve problems, however,

identifying symptoms or harms isn't enough. We also must be able to identify the cause or causes of the problem. Causes are *why* something happens. Establishing causal relationships is difficult and must be done with care. If we solve for the wrong causes, we don't eliminate the harms.

We often have trouble identifying causes. The topic of voter registration is a case in point. An argument has been made that voters must show proof of citizenship before voting to reduce voter fraud. If we want to solve problems associated with voter fraud, however, shouldn't we attempt to discover *why* people may be committing voter fraud? This is a controversial topic with far-reaching economic, social, and political implications. The same can be said of many topics. Laying blame is easy. Finding underlying causes is more difficult—and more important.

When preparing a policy speech that asks you to solve for harms, you should look for any contributing causes. In doing this, you might be able to identify the actual causes. Those who counterargue often cite **alternative causality** when attempting to negate a proposal. Alternative causes may be present in many instances. Persuasive speakers would do well to discover alternative causes rather than simply taking a preferred position.

If you find that any of these alternative causes might contribute to the problem, a plan can solve for them. Causality too often is argued simply, and simple plans result. Simple plans that fail to account for underlying causes do not eliminate harms, and additional harms likely will occur.

A Plan

The thesis for this type of persuasive speech is a general **proposition of policy** that you are advocating. You want the policy to be adopted. The next step in strategically forwarding your most persuasive argument for change is to develop a plan of action that will solve for the causes, thereby eliminating the indictments.

To develop a successful plan, you must consider two basic questions:

1. Is the plan *desirable*? To be desirable, a plan must eliminate the causes of the existing problem. Just as important, the plan must not be the cause of a new problem. For example, some people advocate that voters must present a valid driver's license to vote; however, many people do not

drive and as a result do not have a license. The harm remains, and arguably, new harms, such as denying American citizens the right to participate in the democratic process, may result.

2. Is the plan *practical*? A major concern here is *enforcement*. The plan should include a provision about what will happen if the plan is not followed.

When formulating a plan to solve the problems you have discovered, you must include the means to enforce the plan. Without *enforcement*, a plan is a hollow promise of things that might be better. Basically, your strategy must include a way to encourage or require people to comply with the plan.

A second consideration when designing a plan is *financing*. Everything from rebuilding roads and bridges to security lighting on campus has to be paid for. If you follow the workings of Congress, your state legislature, or even your school's student association, you know that funding is a crucial issue. Presenting a way to finance your plan is a key to persuading an audience. Few of us like to pay for things if we don't have to, and this is especially true of things that don't affect us directly. If we can design a plan that can be funded fairly, chances of success are greater.

Plans also should be developed to satisfy the *special-interest groups* that are involved. These groups may be small, or they may be large, such as the National Rifle Association (NRA), the National Association for the Advancement of Colored People (NAACP), or the National Organization for Women (NOW). Special-interest groups are highly influential in legislative decisions. The Christian Coalition, for example, lobbies on behalf of conservative Protestants. The Susan G. Komen for the Cure Foundation provides education and support for breast cancer research. The American Civil Liberties Union promotes individual rights and liberties. Special-interest groups, large and small, influence policy. When developing a plan, your goal should be to accommodate the needs of pertinent special-interest groups while solving the problems.

A plan also should include *confirming research*, documenting similar plans that have been used elsewhere. Often, individual states or localities will implement a plan that works. If your research reveals this, you can incorporate it, or parts of it, into your plan.

Plans, or laws, that have been implemented successfully elsewhere are called **model legislation**.

Because they have proven to be successful, they become examples for other entities confronted with similar problems. Your research often will reveal policies that work, and these can become a basis for your own plan.

Model Legislation

Model legislation is acts or laws that have been developed in other places, at other times, or by organizations that provide a framework, or model, that can be adopted or replicated by other agencies. Consider this example of model legislation:

On November 13, 2008, The United Nations Division for the Advancement of Women and the United Nations Office on Drugs and Crime issued the report of an expert group meeting entitled, "Good practices in legislation on violence against women." The report contains a new framework for legislation on violence against women, which addresses implementation, monitoring, and evaluation, definitions of violence against women, prevention, protection, investigations and legal proceedings, protection orders, sentencing, family law cases involving violence against women, civil lawsuits, and violence against women and asylum law.

The concerns in the above example deal with the practicality of a plan. Concern for practicality will help you develop a detailed plan that implements the proposition. You are trying to determine if your plan is better than any of the alternatives. If you can convince yourself that the research is complete and that the plan is a good one, you probably have developed a workable plan. Plans are designed to solve existing problems and to avoid future problems. We realize that this is an idealistic situation, but public speaking strategies should allow for the best possible choices, including policy options.

As you can see, policy speaking involves persuading sudiences about facts and values. Your goal, at least implicitly, is to convince an audience of the value of a proposition based on your interpretation of the facts. You are implementing your goal in a persuasive policy speech.

Enforcing a Plan

Legislation by various states was enacted during the 2012 general election in regard to voter identification; however, in some instances it proved difficult to enforce and in other instances states withdrew or modified enactment of the legislation. In short, early legislation proved difficult to enforce and subject to legal challenges.

Justification for the Plan

A plan or policy is only as good as the **justification** generated for it. A plan should not stand alone. An argument should be made for its workability, thereby justifying the plan. If you examine some of the personal choices you have made, you probably will see that these "policies" were accompanied by some justification. Often justification is so powerful that people adopt the policy. Without justifying the solution, you allow the audience to consider alternatives and perhaps reject your solution. The justification step in the speech is a positive strategic choice.

The justification phase of the speech essentially is an argument that the plan will work. This can be done in several ways. First, you can cite analogous situations in which a similar plan has worked. An **analogy** compares an unknown (your plan) to a known situation. With that information, you can argue that your proposed plan worked previously in a known situation. The argument concludes by stating that your plan, being similar, will also work.

When arguing by analogy, you have several options. For instance, you can analyze similar plans that have worked in other countries. If the situations are indeed analogous, a plan that works in another country should work in the United States. The following analogies have been used:

- Other countries impose tariffs on U.S. products; therefore, the United States can successfully do the same.

- England has national health insurance, so it will work in the United States.

These brief statements contain arguments by analogy. Your persuasive strategies include using the best evidence possible and testing the argument to be sure that the analogous situations actually exist.

You also can draw analogies between states. This analogy was mentioned when discussing child restraints in automobiles. A plan used in one state provides the basis for another state's plan or a national plan. Therefore, you can use model legislation as a basis for the plan and its justification. Examples of state analogies are:

- Illinois enacted mandatory minimum nutritional guidelines for school lunches; South Dakota should adopt these same guidelines.

- Most states fund government through a state income tax. A state income tax here would increase general funds, too.

As with any argument, these analogies are subject to verification and must withstand the scrutiny of the audience, which is prepared to analyze the reasoning involved.

You also could develop analogies based on smaller governmental jurisdictions. If a city or county has a plan that works and you adopt it, its justification stems from an analogy. If a college or other agency with the power to mandate some action has had successes in implementing policies, these are analogous situations.

Many people also develop analogies by discussing what has happened in the past. They argue that the plans formulated previously are better than existing plans. In effect, they argue that newer plans created other harms that would be remedied by returning to the policies of the past. Consider this example:

> The economic programs enacted between 1933 and 1936, called the New Deal, focused on what was called the "3 Rs": Relief, Recovery, and Reform, relief for the unemployed and poor; recovery of the economy to normal levels; and reform of the financial system to prevent a repeat depression.

Other examples will come to mind. In any case, the idea is clear. Returning to past policies may have advantages, and a successful strategy can be developed by analyzing pertinent policies of the past.

You will have to be careful when using analogies to justify the plan, keeping some criteria in mind.

1. The analogy must be *relevant*. That is why we mention the concept of model legislation.

2. Because analogies usually come from research, they must be *current, comprehensive,* and from a *credible* source of information.

3. The analogy must *make sense*. An audience member hearing the analogy should be able to accept it based on its nature as evidence and because it isn't too far-fetched to believe.

You also may choose to justify your plan by using expert opinion about the plan—by using **testimony** from research sources. The expert cited in support of the plan must be credible, the evidence should be comprehensive, and the testimony must be current.

Finding testimony to support a plan is not as difficult as it may seem at first. When you are developing the plan, you often will find that those who propose change are also the experts who can show that the plan will work. Justification should be specific to the plan you are proposing, or specific to the existing plans you are using as models for your own policies.

The best justification for any plan is that it eliminates the harms, indictments, or causes you have identified. You may cite analogous situations or testimony in proving that the problems will be eliminated.

Lacking evidence to prove that a plan is justified, you must create the justification through argument. This means that you must develop a rational explanation to show that the harms will be eliminated. This is a much more difficult task than finding evidence to support the justification.

Let's suppose your speech is about improving wildlife habitat. For the sake of argument, let's also suppose that no evidence is available to support the justification for, or benefits of, habitat improvement. The speech structure might look like this:

I. Wildlife habitat is decreasing.
II. Habitat loss is caused by three things.
III. The government should take three steps to improve wildlife habitat.
IV. Habitat loss can be prevented.
   A. Developers will not pursue marginal land without government incentives.
   B. Long-term land-use plans will provide for habitat protection.
   C. A public education program will increase awareness of the benefits of habitat.

Point IV shows how a justification would be developed when you lack evidence to support the claims. Each of the subpoints requires additional explanation, just as any substructure element in any

speech. In this example, however, evidence does not support your argumentative claims. Your analysis supports the claims.

Although you can prove, through evidence and analysis, that a plan is justified, without sufficient evidence you must prove that the plan will alleviate the harms. This can be done by your analysis, but it is more difficult than using evidence and may invite more critical analysis. In any case, you must prove the workability of the plan.

The outline on the wildlife topic could take this form:

I. Wildlife habitat is decreasing.
   A. Wetlands are being drained.
   B. Deforestation is occurring.
   C. Cities are expanding.
II. The habitat loss has three causes.
   A. Government incentives encourage development.
   B. State tax laws encourage development.
   C. Local governments fail to regulate expansions.
III. The government should take three steps to solve the problem.
   A. It should rescind legislation allowing development.
   B. State and local governments should require long-term land-use plans.
   C. A federally funded public awareness plan should be enacted.
IV. Habitat loss can be prevented.
   A. Developers will not pursue marginal land without incentives.
   B. Long-term land-use plans will provide for habitat protection.
   C. A public education program will increase awareness of the benefits of habitat.

The finished outline is simple, yet when supported by evidence and analysis, the audience is exposed to a strong, persuasive speech about wildlife habitat.

Summary

We are exposed to persuasive appeals almost every day. Health-care providers encourage us to control our diet and exercise. Organizations ask us to join and support their efforts. Politicians ask us to vote. Persuasive appeals can be based on questions of fact, questions of value, and questions of policy.

In this chapter we concentrate on the policy speech because policy speaking most often affects us in our daily lives. If you can construct and present a policy speech using the strategies presented in this book, you will become a more informed analyst of the policies that affect you.

Persuasive speaking is built on the same foundation as informative speaking. Before researching the speech, you must select and narrow a topic. Your thesis sentence has the same function as it does for the informative thesis. You should employ research strategies so you ultimately can select the strongest presentation.

You must deliver the speech in a manner appropriate to the occasion. Basic public speaking strategies are applicable to various types of speeches. As the goal of the speech changes, implementation of the strategies may change.

Persuasion may be the most complex speaking you do. It requires special attention to analysis of evidence. Persuasion is based more strongly on values than other types of speaking. Therefore, your analysis must be more thorough. Audience members may agree or disagree with you. A strong persuasive speech can accommodate varying audience values.

Review Items: Chapter 12

Name _____ Date _____

1. What is persuasive speaking?

2. How does persuasive speaking differ from informative speaking?

3. What are questions of fact?

4. What are questions of value?

5. What are questions of policy?

6. What are the four major elements of a policy speech?

1.

2.

3.

4.

7. What are indictments?

8. Why does this chapter concentrate on the causes of indictments?

9. What are the essential components of a plan?

10. How is a plan justified?

Public Speaking and Small-Group Strategy

13

Humans have a basic need to belong, and groups help fill that need. Our needs vary, though, so we become members of different kinds of groups to meet our individual needs. Groups can be classified into two major types—primary and secondary. **Primary groups** provide us with the basic needs to ensure survival. Examples of primary groups are family, friends, roommates, churches, and college classmates. Our association with primary groups usually is long-term, perhaps even lifelong. We belong to these groups because they help us establish relationships that give us love, comfort, support, and a sense of belonging.

Secondary groups, by contrast, are formulated for the purpose of completing a task. Examples of secondary groups are student body councils, parent advisory associations, county commissions, and business and commerce organizations.

Small groups are becoming increasingly popular in our culture. We should study the dynamics of small groups for the following reasons:

1. Groups are not merely a collection of individuals. They are separate and distinct units with characteristics and behaviors unique to those units.

2. The decisions reached within a small-group setting have a direct impact on our everyday lives.

3. Small-group interactions influence individuals within the group. What we do and say within these groups affects us both as individuals and as a group.

4. We have a responsibility to ourselves and the community to become better informed about participation in small groups and to become trained in working in and leading small groups. This requires strong public speaking skills in the small-group setting.

Characteristics of Small Groups

A working definition of **small group** is "a limited number of persons engaged in face-to-face interaction in an effort to achieve some interdependent goal." Looking at this definition point by point, we can develop a list of criteria that apply to small groups.

1. Small groups are composed of 3 to 15 members, with an average of 7 or 8 members.

2. When members of a group are involved in face-to-face interaction, this interaction must be spontaneous in contrast to prepared, set speeches. Group members react, adapt, and respond to each other.

3. Small-group participants desire to achieve an interdependent goal. This means that all members depend on each other for the ultimate success or failure of their overall effort. This interdependence also fosters a sense of cooperation and, ultimately, belonging.

4. Looking at the last word in our definition, we can see that groups desire to do something. Groups have a purpose and direct their activities to achieve their goals.

> ## Main Characteristics of Small Groups
> 1. Limited size of 3 to 15 members
> 2. Absence of set speeches
> 3. Interdependence in regard to group outcome
> 4. Goal orientation

Advantages of Group Processes

The major advantage of working within groups is the opportunity to generate more ideas and points of view. This multiplied experience compounds resources and also increases the number of potential solutions available. Group processes, too, provide a better end product or decision. Group interaction generally enhances the refinement and detailing of decisions. It fits the old adage that two (or in the case of small groups, three or more) heads are better than one.

On a personal level, working in groups enables the individual to satisfy the need for social acceptance and to accept decisions more readily as a result of being involved in the decision-making process. Perhaps even more important, involvement in small groups offers participants the chance to refine and improve their communication skills. Most people feel comfortable expressing their views and ideas in a small-group setting, and they participate freely.

Disadvantages of Group Processes

The group process has several inherent problems. For one thing, groups can be inefficient. When interacting, people are tempted to get off the subject or task at hand. This can be a serious impediment in light of the time-limited nature of groups. Because it takes longer to come to a group decision than to an individual decision, it is important to make the best use of available time.

Another drawback of working in groups is a phenomenon called **groupthink**, in which one or more individuals who hold a minority opinion either remain silent or agree verbally with the group.[1] This may result when an individual does not want to rock the boat or wants to expedite the process and get the task completed. Some people feel self-conscious or apprehensive about expressing their own views. When groupthink is operating, potential ideas, solutions, or viewpoints that could be beneficial in producing a decision are suppressed or withheld.

Still another disadvantage of group work becomes apparent if the group norms are not held by all. Group members may clash over differing values or rules. If these values or beliefs are strongly held, conflict sometimes develops, that could prevent the group from staying on task.

Types of Secondary Groups

The four basic kinds of secondary groups are self-help, study or learning, information sharing, and problem solving.

1. SELF-HELP GROUPS are those developed for our personal enhancement. These groups provide support for various personal problems and concerns. Groups have been formed for drug rehabilitation, single parents, stress management, and eating disorders, to name just a few.

2. STUDY OR LEARNING GROUPS meet to share knowledge and experience. You may belong to this type of group already without even realizing it. Perhaps you and three or four friends get together to study for chemistry exams. Other examples of study groups are seminars and tutoring sessions or book clubs.

3. INFORMATION-SHARING GROUPS are formed to engage in research and data gathering on a specific topic. These groups do not necessarily make decisions or reach solutions. Perhaps your school is exploring the possibility of creating

---

1 J. K. Brilhart and G. J. Galanes, *Effective Group Discussion*, 6th ed. (Dubuque, Iowa: Wm. C. Brown, Publishers, 1989).

a nonalcoholic pub on campus. A committee might be formed to study the feasibility of the project. The group will have to find out if there is a demand for this type of establishment, where it might be located, how it would be financed, and who would manage the facility.

4. PROBLEM-SOLVING GROUPS have the goal of researching a problem thoroughly, considering all pertinent facts, and then developing a solution to the problem. This type of group is becoming more and more evident in our communities and businesses. It is the one on which we will concentrate here.

Problem Solving in the Small Group

Participants in a group may be required to contribute to solving a problem or developing a solution to a problematic situation. Let us assume that, as a member of an introductory speech class, you have been assigned to a problem-solving group that must select a topic, research the subject area, and then participate in a group presentation to the class. Upon meeting the members of your assigned group, you choose a topic for consideration and select a group leader.

At this point a lot of work has to be done to complete this task—work that requires organization. Your group must adopt a workable and dependable model to help structure your efforts. This will enable you as an individual and a participant within the group to organize and keep your group on the right track.

The model we will use here is John Dewey's **reflective thinking model**. It consists of five steps:

1. Locate and define the question.
2. Analyze the question.
3. Generate possible solutions.
4. Choose the best solution.
5. Implement the solution.

By following each step in the reflective thinking model, a group will find it easier to develop an agenda or outline to help structure the problem-solving efforts. Specific kinds of information are structured in each of the five steps.

Locating and Defining the Problem

In the first step the group is asked to pinpoint the problem. Terms, concepts, and ideas within the topic area are defined and clarified. Careful attention during this step enables a group to direct energy to the

problem and to concentrate the research. It generates explanations that keep the discussion on target.

The first task of the small group is to put the topic in a question format. Typically, the topic is structured in the form of a **question of policy** when dealing with a contemporary problem. This is a question that asks for a general solution or a plan of action. The topic always must be in question form and must be kept free of words that contain bias. It also must be open ended, not lending itself readily to a yes or no answer, as well as singular in nature, asking only one question at a time.

Representative examples of policy questions are:

● What should be the U.S. government policy in regard to aid to education?

● To what extent should the U.S. government subsidize agricultural products?

● What can the U.S. government do to reduce the rate of prescription drug overdose?

● What can be done to change the policy of the U.S. government in regard to eminent domain?

Second, the group may decide to place limitations on the discussion. This process is similar to that of narrowing a topic during speech preparation. For instance, assume that a discussion group is researching the topic of aid to education. The group may decide to limit discussion on this topic to aid for higher education. Another way to limit the topic would be to narrow the discussion to student loans. Narrowing the topic makes it more manageable in terms of the assignment and time constraints. Limitations could be topical, spatial, or chronological. The potential areas of limiting a discussion are numerous and unique to each topic.

Finally, the group may want to define certain terms, words, or phrases relevant to the discussion. If we apply this step to the topic of aid to education, the group may want to define the term *education*. Other terms that might be defined include, for example, *higher education* and *technical education*.

Definitions may be of two different types:

1. Textbook or printed—documenting definitions from a dictionary, book, or other reliable printed source.

2. Operational—creating definitions for the purpose of the discussion or assignment at hand.

Whatever the choice, the group should define any words or terminology that may be ambiguous and possibly interfere with the clarity and progress of the discussion.

Analyzing the Question

The second step takes into account all relevant facts. Here the group will be able to determine if, and to what extent, a problem exists. You may ask the question, "How many people does this problem affect?" You also might ask, "How much financial, societal, or moral harm will result from this problem?" Beyond thinking of *harmful effects*, a situation or problem may have offsetting *positive effects* that will be important to analyze and consider. Finally, ask what will happen if this problem is not resolved.

The second area to analyze is *cause*. What is producing these harmful effects? What is causing the problem? What factors have contributed to this problem? Have similar situations happened in other places or at other times? The group should try to discover as much background information on the problem as possible to be better able to develop realistic criteria for possible solutions and avoid a common error as the discussion progresses: Quite often small groups rush into possible solutions before adequately investigating the effects and causes surrounding a problem. Without a firm grasp of the causes, a solution to the problem will be elusive.

During the analysis step of problem solving, the group is required to do research. This research will parallel the research process used when developing a speech. All aspects of the topic area have to be researched thoroughly.

Generating Possible Solutions

To generate possible solutions requires that the group begin to look at possible solutions to the problem the members have been researching. With each member of the group armed with facts and evidence that provide background, the group can begin to come up with realistic solutions to eliminate the problem.

An effective way for groups to approach this step is **brainstorming**. This technique provides an avenue for generating a great number of possible solutions at one time while withholding critical evaluation until the brainstorming is complete. To get started, someone in the group agrees or is assigned to record all ideas as other members begin to offer ideas. This technique allows every member to contribute not only once but perhaps several times. The rules to observe are as follows:

1. Everyone is encouraged to participate.
2. Every idea is accepted.
3. Evaluation or judgment of ideas is not permitted.
4. Quantity, not quality, is emphasized.
5. No set speeches are allowed.

These simple rules allow a group to generate a wide variety of ideas that may ignite overlapping and expanded ideas.

Choosing the Best Solution

Once all ideas have been exhausted, the group looks at the list of alternative solutions and begins to critically evaluate the merits and drawbacks of each potential solution. At this point the group should keep in mind the causes and harmful effects uncovered in Step 2. The list of causes and effects should be applied to each solution generated in brainstorming. This list contains the criteria that will help develop an organized approach in the evaluation process and also will increase the probability of selecting the best possible solution.

Arriving at a solution acceptable to all group members may be difficult. In an attempt to avoid potential conflict during this discussion:

1. Avoid personalities; deal with the issues.
2. Emphasize common ground among group members; stress points of agreement.
3. Keep an open mind to all ideas and suggestions.
4. Remember the task the group is trying to complete; don't lose sight of the goal.

These guidelines should help the group come to a consensus when selecting the final solution. Consensus is reached when all members of the group embrace an idea or solution with varying degrees of acceptance or enthusiasm. Some members of the group may endorse a solution wholeheartedly, and other members might view the solution as barely adequate.

Implementing the Solution

The final step in the model concentrates on the specifics of putting the chosen plan into action. In an effort to produce a smooth transition from paper solution to actual solution, the group will have to address a number of questions. The best way to approach this step is to develop a list of organizational questions that the group can answer. Some of these questions might be:

- 👤 Who should implement this plan? What agency or organization is most capable of administering the plan?

- 👤 How much will this plan cost? Where can the funds come from? What special equipment or materials will be needed?

- 👤 How easily can this plan of action be implemented?

- 👤 How can we monitor or evaluate the effectiveness of the plan?

Once the group has answered questions pertinent to implementing the plan, it will have to be presented to the public, class, or business that assigned this task to your group.

Formats for Group Presentations

At times reports take the form of written papers. At other times they take the form of an oral presentation by the group or some members of the group. A number of formats can be used for these presentations, depending on the needs of the group and the audience.

If your group is required to make an oral presentation of its research or findings, a format for the oral presentation must be chosen. Because this is a public presentation, the needs of your listening audience must be considered. The four types of group presentation formats are panel, symposium, colloquium, and forum. Whichever method is chosen, the key point to remember is that this presentation is being made for the audience's information, education, and pleasure.

Panel

A **panel discussion** usually begins with a moderator or group leader introducing the topic question. Panel members then interact, respond, and discuss the topic based on their knowledge and expertise. The group leader directs the panel, asking follow-up questions and using an outline or agenda to keep the discussion on track. The group leader also keeps notes and summarizes topic areas.

A key feature of this format is the absence of set speeches. The members participate spontaneously. The moderator encourages participation from all members. Preparation and organization are important to a successful outcome. After discussion on the topic has been exhausted, the moderator usually opens the discussion to questions from the audience.

Symposium

A **symposium** differs from a panel discussion in that the symposium consists of a series of set speeches by each member of the group. Each speech may deal with a specific aspect of the topic, or perhaps several members offer individual concerns and other members suggest alternatives or solutions. Generally, each group structures its symposium based on the topic. A symposium format is useful when trying to inform or present facts. After the symposium presentation, the audience may ask questions and participate with the symposium members.

Colloquium

In a **colloquium** format the audience asks questions of a panel of experts. Usually, the announced topic is the only area discussed. Audience members can direct questions to a specific member of the panel. One drawback of this format is that the panel members cannot interact with each other, and as a result, only areas that are questioned are addressed. This format is most useful for information sharing.

Forum

A **forum** is the most open ended and least structured form of public discussion. Forums enable entire audiences to participate in the information-sharing, decision-making process. An example of this format is the **town meeting**, in which people are able to debate and discuss ideas, responding to each other's ideas and proposing solutions. Issues then are put to a vote of the assembly.

The moderator of a forum has quite a job. He or she has to follow an agenda, maintain order, be fair in allowing participation by all members wishing to do so, and provide an opportunity for all points of view to be expressed. The moderator also has to summarize and clarify information. A parliamentary process may have to be used to maintain order and ensure progress. If this is the case, the moderator should have some background in parliamentary procedure.

Leadership in Small Groups

The first task of any group is to decide who will assume a leadership role. Notice the word *leadership* rather than *leader*. A leader implies a person, whereas

leadership denotes a role or function. A great deal of research on leadership has been done over the years. Leaders can be appointed or elected, but they also can evolve or emerge. Leadership can be situational, with different people taking on the role in given situations. Whatever the method used to designate the group's leadership, groups should determine who will fill this position. Without a person in the leadership role, it will be difficult to organize and complete the assigned task.

Leadership in small groups entails organizing and directing groups in completing some task. It is a multifaceted role. An effective group leader can be one of the single-most important factors in the success of the group.

Group leaders initially may be overwhelmed by the magnitude of responsibilities they must take on. The job will be more manageable if we look at the overall responsibility and separate the leadership role as having three functions: administrative, facilitative, and correlative.

Administrative Function

The group leader may be responsible for scheduling the times and meeting places. In addition, the group leader is in charge of contacting group members, distributing outlines and agendas, making assignments, and delegating responsibilities. The group leader begins all meetings, takes notes, and at the conclusion of the meeting summarizes what took place and informs the group members of the next areas or tasks to be started.

Facilitative Function

In facilitating the group, the leader directs the group's efforts during the actual planning, research, and presentation of the group discussion. The leader discusses all issues facing the group, attempts to solicit the views and opinions of all group members, and helps to keep the group efforts organized and on track.

Further, the group leader helps set the pace and provides the tempo to keep the discussion moving. In addition, the leader poses follow-up questions, asks for clarification, takes notes, and summarizes final areas of consensus and solution. Perhaps one of the most important traits of a leader, in addition to organizational skills, is the ability to listen carefully and respond to what is said in the group.

Correlative Function

The correlative function of leadership concerns group interaction and how the group develops on an interpersonal level. The leader must be prepared to deal with potential conflict among group members. The group leader tries to understand what motivates members and to determine how prepared the members are to participate. The leader also must approach all members fairly and equally and try to develop group cohesion. An asset of a group leader is sensitivity to the needs and feelings of each member, working out differences of opinion and establishing areas of common ground.

Participation in Small-Group Discussion

Every member of a small group will have to assume responsibilities toward completing the group's task. A successful group experience requires the cooperation and effort of each member. Members can ensure the success of the group in four ways:

1. Participate actively.

2. Avoid conflict.

3. Follow through with assignments.

4. Commit to the group task.

Active Participation

Involvement of every member in all phases of the group task is essential. Withholding ideas and energy denies the group the chance to look at alternative solutions, ideas, and suggestions. Members should openly encourage each other to share ideas, because some members of the group will be shy or reluctant to get involved. Others like to talk about their ideas and information so much that they can end up dominating the group. We have to tell ourselves to listen carefully to what each member is saying and not saying. The ideal group discussion has balanced participation in which all members participate equally. This is a difficult goal, but one worth striving for.

Follow-Through with Assignments

When members are assigned a group task, they must complete the job. This means being on time for meetings, providing an outline based on personal research, arranging interviews, or contacting group members. Whatever the job, the group is counting on each member to help complete the task and assume his or her fair share of responsibility to ensure a successful outcome.

Avoidance of Conflict

At times, conflict within the group is nearly unavoidable, especially when dealing with a problem-solving question. Members may have strong opinions and beliefs. If anything, a certain amount of disagreement is beneficial to ensure a quality product. Members should avoid personality clashes, though—comments that are insensitive or counterproductive—and try to focus on the group task instead of individuals. Compromise may become essential in satisfactory group experiences.

Commitment to Group Task

Whatever the motivation, whatever task the group is performing, group members must commit their energy and resources to the group effort. If each member commits himself or herself to the group undertaking, positive behaviors are likely to emerge. Participants will find themselves cooperating and developing a sense of unity. Conflicts are likely to diminish, and members will feel a sense of satisfaction with their group effort. A strong commitment by all members will ensure an outcome or a finished product that can be a source of pride, and they will be assured that they have created the best possible solution or plan.

Public Speaking and Small-Group Discussion: A Synthesis

A correlation can be drawn between the public speaking experience and participation in small-group discussions. Many skills developed for public speaking are integrated in the small-group experience. These skills will help you be a more proficient and welcome participant in a group effort.

The most noticeable skills deal with the various facets of speech preparation. When working with a topic for group consideration, you have to narrow and define, as well as apply limitations, to your discussion. This resembles the narrowing of a topic for a speech. Also, you should organize or arrange the topic areas that you will cover during small-group discussion. This procedure is similar to developing an organization for an informative or persuasive speech.

The research that you undertake in developing a speech follows the same process that members of a group use when preparing for a public discussion. All rules of documentation, use of evidence, and analysis are observed in both cases. If you are to make a public presentation of your group findings, you must consider the audience and its needs and make adaptations to the listening public.

As in the public speaking situation, you will make use of listening skills in small-group discussions, listening and reacting to a great number of messages and kinds of information. These critical listening skills will serve you and the group as a whole in approaching the problem and selecting the best possible solution.

Finally, you must consider your role as an advocate for the plan or solution your group agrees upon. You will have to incorporate all the skills of persuasive speaking to ensure adoption and implementation of the group's recommendation. You will have to use all available resources, evidence, and types of reasoning to represent your positions adequately. In this role you have the opportunity to present and further improve your expanding delivery skills.

Summary

Small groups are becoming more prevalent in our society. Small groups are characterized by 3 to 15 people who interrelate in completing some kind of task. Advantages of group processes include the generation of more ideas and the potential for better-quality decisions, along with social enhancement and improved communication skills. Some disadvantages of small groups are that they are time consuming, members tend to get off the subject, they may fall into a pattern of groupthink, and cultural norms may clash.

Secondary groups are of four types: self-help groups, study groups, information-sharing groups, and problem-solving groups. Problem-solving groups can be facilitated by adopting John Dewey's reflective thinking model, which uses five steps: (1) location and definition, (2) analysis, (3) generating possible solutions, (4) choosing the best solution, and (5) implementing the solution. Group formats include the panel discussion, symposium, colloquium, and forum.

Groups will operate more efficiently with someone in the leadership role. Leaders may be designated, they might be implied, or they may emerge from the group. Leadership roles and functions are those of administrator, facilitator, and correlator. Participation in groups also carries responsibility. Four areas of responsibility are thorough participation, commitment to the group, positive interaction, and completion of assigned tasks.

Throughout the group process you will use many of the skills you learn in public-speaking training. You also will have the opportunity to be an advocate for the group and to improve your communication skills.

Review Items: Chapter 13

Name _____ Date _____

1. Why do we belong to groups?

2. What are primary groups? Secondary groups? Designate the groups you belong to as one of these two types.

3. What are the four characteristics of small groups?
   1. _____
   2. _____
   3. _____
   4. _____

4. What are the advantages of small groups?

5. What are some disadvantages of small groups?

6. What are the types of secondary groups?

7. Explain Dewey's reflective thinking model.

8. What are the major formats for group presentations?

9. What are the leadership roles and functions in the small group?

10. What are the responsibilities of group participants?

Personal Inventory

Name _____

Using the following categories, write down as many topics as you can that represent experiences you have had. Use this inventory to help you in selecting topics for your speeches.

BACKGROUND: (hometown, family, ethnic, and religious history)

_____

_____

_____

_____

_____

WORK EXPERIENCE:

_____

_____

_____

_____

_____

HOBBIES AND INTERESTS:

_____

_____

_____

_____

_____

SKILLS AND TALENTS:

_____

_____

_____

_____

_____

TRAVEL:

_____

_____

_____

_____

_____

ACADEMIC AND EXTRACURRICULAR/COCURRICULAR INTERESTS:

_____

_____

_____

_____

_____

UNIQUE EXPERIENCES:

_____

_____

_____

_____

_____

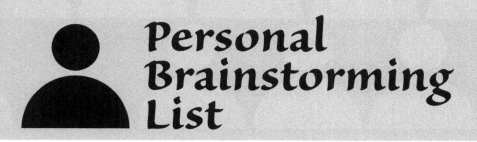

Personal Brainstorming List

Use the following list to create possible topics for speeches.

PEOPLE:

_____

_____

_____

_____

_____

_____

_____

_____

ANIMALS:

_____

_____

_____

_____

_____

_____

_____

_____

OBJECTS:

_____

_____

_____

_____

_____

_____

_____

_____

PLACES:

_____

_____

_____

_____

_____

_____

_____

_____

STRUCTURES:

_____

_____

_____

_____

_____

_____

_____

_____

_____

_____

EVENTS:

_____

_____

_____

_____

_____

_____

_____

_____

_____

_____

CONCEPTS:

_____

_____

_____

_____

_____

_____

_____

_____

_____

_____

PROCESS OR PROCEDURE:

_____

_____

_____

_____

_____

_____

_____

_____

_____

_____

Speech Assignments

Speech Assignment 1: Personal Attitude

This speech on personal attitude is intended to be an icebreaker. Over the years, you have formulated ideas and attitudes that you want to communicate publicly to others. Often you have little or no chance to express these beliefs in an academic setting where they can be analyzed and discussed. As a consequence, your opinions often are part of your daily communication without your own reflective thinking or others' analysis.

This introductory assignment also gives you the opportunity to become acquainted with your classmates' beliefs. This will help you analyze your audience so you can better relate your ideas to that audience in future speeches.

Like all assignments, this speech should be a well-thought-out, carefully structured presentation. Preparing it must not be put off until the last minute, because procrastination will result in a trivial thesis, hasty analysis, poor structure, and weak delivery, which may increase your fear of the speaking situation. Careful forethought and practice are the keys to reducing speech anxiety or communication apprehension.

Specifically, this assignment asks you to do the following.

1. Prepare a speech explaining one of your attitudes that you would like others to understand.

2. Develop a thesis statement ("I believe…."). Write it where indicated on the outline (three times).

3. List three reasons you believe as you do. These are the main points in the body of your outline (directly support the thesis).

4. Prepare supporting examples from your past experience or prior reading, explaining each main point (called subpoints).

5. Prepare an introduction and a conclusion.

6. Prepare an outline note card (maximum 20 words).

7. Practice your speech aloud several times.

8. Submit a draft outline to be checked in class.

9. Turn in two copies of the outline to the instructor on the day you speak.

10. Adhere to a three-minute time frame for the speech.

11. Deliver the speech extemporaneously.

12. Turn in a checklist and grading rubric on the day you speak.

Personal Attitude Outline Worksheet

Name: _____

Thesis: "I believe _____."

Introduction

I. Gain interest and attention

II. State thesis: "I believe...."

Body

I. First reason for believing as you do.

A. Personal experience examples.

B. Prior reading, etc.

II. Second reason

A.

B.

III. Third reason

A.

B.

Conclusion

I. Summary of ideas

II. Restatement of thesis

Note: This outline format is required for all outlines in this class. Your outlines are to be in sentence form, as you will see in the following sample outlines.

Personal Attitude Speech Sample Outline

Personal Attitude Speech
Speaker Name: _____

Thesis statement: I believe that all college freshmen should use a planner.

Introduction

    I. College life can be extremely overwhelming.

    II. I believe that all college freshmen should use a planner.

Body

    I. Planners help keep students organized.

        A. All coursework and exams can be clearly noted.

        B. All social events and activities can be easily scheduled.

    II. Planners help to decrease stress.

        A. A clear plan promotes a calm mind.

        B. A clear plan promotes an organized routine.

    III. Planner use sets up students for future success.

        A. Planner use will be useful in future semesters.

        B. Planner use will be useful in future careers.

Conclusion

    I. Planners offer organization, help to decrease stress, and can set up students for future success.

    II. I believe that all college freshmen should use a planner.

Speaker's Note Card

Introduction

    I. Overwhelming

    II. Thesis

Body

    I. Organized

        A. Work and exams

        B. Events and activities

    II. Decrease stress

        A. Calm

        B. Routine

    III. Success

        A. Future courses

        B. Career

Conclusion

    I. Summary

    II. Thesis

Checklist: Personal Attitude Speech

❑ Have you chosen a topic you are comfortable with?

❑ Have you developed a thesis statement ("I believe…") and written it where instructed?

❑ Have you listed three reasons (main points) you believe the way you do?

❑ Do you have personal supporting information for each subpoint?

❑ Have you prepared an introduction and a conclusion?

❑ Has the instructor checked your draft outline?

❑ Do you have two copies of the outline prepared for the day you speak and your checklist and grading rubric ready to hand in?

❑ Have you written the outline in complete sentences throughout, including the introduction and conclusion?

❑ Have you prepared one note card with no more than 20 words?

❑ Have you rehearsed the speech, and is it three minutes long?

❑ Have you rehearsed the delivery for an extemporaneous speech?

❑ Is the thesis statement stated orally after the introduction?

❑ Have you followed the outline format used in this assignment?

❑ Have you practiced establishing eye contact with the audience, using the note card only for references?

❑ Are you prepared to speak in an animated, conversational voice?

❑ In your practice, did you avoid vocal clutter (um, you know, ah, well, okay)?

❑ Have you practiced enough to communicate your ideas fluently?

Personal Attitude Speech Rubric

Speaker: _____ Grade (out of 100 points): _____

(Key: E = Excellent, G = Good, A = Average, F = Fair, P = Poor)

Outline & Note Cards

Followed the prescribed outline format	E G A F P
Used complete declarative sentences for each point on the outline	E G A F P
Used no more than 20 words on the outline note card	E G A F P
Turned in two copies of the outline on the date of the speech	E G A F P
Turned in the completed checklist for this assignment	E G A F P

Invention

Tailored and adapted message to audience and the occasion	E G A F P
Achieved the general purpose of the assignment	E G A F P
Stayed within the prescribed assignment time limit	E G A F P
Developed a clear and concisely worded thesis statement	E G A F P
Achieved reasonably direct and communicative delivery	E G A F P

Introduction

Grabbed attention of audience with unique, attention-getting device	E G A F P
Provided an obvious thesis statement	E G A F P
Previewed main points	E G A F P

Body

Included three main points in the body of the speech	E G A F P
Supported each main point by at least two subordinate points	E G A F P
Supported points with varied personal examples and experiences	E G A F P
Presented main points in a specific order	E G A F P
Made main points have focus and connection to the thesis	E G A F P
Regularly used transitions between the main points	E G A F P

Conclusion

Clearly summarized main point	E G A F P
Restated the thesis	E G A F P
Included no new information	E G A F P

Style

Used acceptable grammar, pronunciation, and clear articulation	E G A F P
Demonstrated an understanding of accuracy, clarity, appropriateness, and vividness in language use	E G A F P

Delivery

Maintained sustained eye contact with the audience	E G A F P
Stayed composed and resisted distractions	E G A F P
Recited speech extemporaneously	E G A F P
Had vocal variety	E G A F P
Had appropriate volume	E G A F P
Used the body as a communicative instrument	E G A F P

General Comments

_____

_____

_____

Speech Assignment 2: Informative Speech

Using language with clarity is an art. It involves choosing and using words that relate best to the speaker's intended purpose and meaning for a specific audience. Words have connotative and denotative meanings. If these meanings express different ideas, audience members will attach whichever meaning they usually associate with the word. When the speaker and the listener agree on the meaning, the communication is effective.

Do you remember a recent experience when you gave directions to someone, or received directions from someone, and still ended up going the wrong way? How about the time you followed those "easy" directions and discovered that the trial-and-error method was less confusing? A lot of informing is always going on, but much of it can be confusing.

This assignment gives you a chance to develop your language and organization skills and reduce the "fuzziness" sometimes attached to messages so your audience will receive your intended meaning and feelings. Good organization of your ideas makes it easier for your audience to understand your speech and will aid you, the speaker, as well.

Your purpose in this assignment is to inform. Perhaps no one can be totally informative, because speakers and audiences both filter information through biases. Still, you can use words carefully, choosing them because they are the best words to carry your intended thoughts to the audience.

The purpose will be carried out by observing the following assignment requirements:

1. The subject of the speech must be
   a. an explanation of a process or procedure; or
   b. a description of an object, place, structure, animal, person, event, or concept.

2. All students must have their topics approved.

3. The major objective of this speech is to convey a clear and thorough understanding of the subject under discussion. It is not intended to be a persuasive speech.

4. The thesis of the speech is a single declarative sentence at the top of the outline and stated after the introduction.

5. The speech must be based on at least five outside sources of information, three of which must be peer-reviewed sources.

6. Evidence from these research resources will be used to support the subpoints.

7. All non-original material, whether quoted or paraphrased, must have oral documentation.

8. The outline requirements from the previous speech apply.

9. A complete reference section should be placed at the bottom of each outline to support your points. Two copies of the outline are to be turned in to the instructor on the day of the speech.

10. The time limit is four to six minutes.

11. Speaker notes are limited to 20 words plus separate notes for quoting supporting materials. (See sample entry.)

12. Visual aids are not allowed for this assignment.

Stating the Thesis Sentence for the Informative Speech

The thesis sentence of any speech must be a single declarative sentence. It provides the central idea you want to present in your speech. You may include in the thesis a partial statement of your main points. Place your thesis sentence at the top of your outline, and announce it again as the last statement of your introduction. Some sample thesis sentences are:

- There are several theories about who were the first immigrants in North America.
- Dinosaur National Monument offers visitors an opportunity to observe billions of years of geological history.
- The street artist Bansky is a graffiti master, painter, and activist.
- Katydids are oblong, winged insects that have undergone a genetic change.

Oral Documentation

1. Oral documentation is the process of giving credit for all non-original materials used in a speech, citing author, title, date of publication, etc.

2. Orally documented material is used to support a subpoint in a speech. It is never a subpoint in itself.

3. Oral documentation does not appear in the outline.

4. Oral documentation should be put on source cards and keyed to an outline card.

5. Students should document as they proceed through the speech. Documentation must be specific—no "blanket" documentation.

6. When documenting a previously used source, the author's last name or the title of the publication will suffice. ("Again, according to Smith . . .")

7. Each subpoint should be supported by at least one piece of documented data.

8. Both copies of the outline should include source-card numbers.

9. Students should practice reading source cards until they are fluent and maintain some eye contact while presenting the data.

10. Verbal credit must be given for all non-original material used in the speech. Any information gained through research (by whatever method) must be documented verbally at the time the information is presented in the speech.

Documentation may take many forms. Some examples are:

"According to *Time* (date), ..."

"According to CNN News (date),..."

"According to an interview with MSNBC host Rachel Maddow on (date) . . ."

Note: Interview documentation should be cited parenthetically in the source cards and not be included in the reference list. Some examples are:

(Jerry L. Ferguson, personal communication, July 31, 2013.)

(Jerry D. Jorgensen, personal communication, August 5, 2013.)

Standard APA formatting says that interviews should not be listed in the reference section, however for the purpose of our Fundamentals of Speech outlines and reference materials, you will be required to include interview references in the reference section of your outlines.

(In its final form, the reference section should be alphabetized according to the first word/letter in the entry.)

Rules for, and examples of, oral documentation will be given in the lecture. Each speech must adhere to these rules.

Sample Reference Entries

The following examples are based on the style of the *Publication Manual of the American Psychological Association, 6th Ed.* (APA). When you are putting your reference list together, alphabetize your entries. The categories below are given only to show the differences in style.

Books

Haleta, L. (2013). *Public Speaking: Strategic Choices* (7th ed.). Englewood, CO: Morton Publishing.

Richmond, V. P., Wrench, J. S, McCroskey, J. C. (2013). *Communication apprehension, avoidance, and effectiveness* (6th ed.). Upper Saddle River, NJ: Pearson.

Periodicals

Kandel, E. R., & Squire, L. R. (2000, November 10). Neuroscience: Breaking down scientific barriers to the study of brain and mind. *Science, 290*, 1113–1120.

Journals

Rubin, R. B., Rubin, A. M., & Jordan, F. F. (1997). Effects of instruction on communication apprehension and communication competence. *Communication Education, 46*, 104–114.

Morreale, S. P., Worley, D.W., & Hugenberg, H. (2010). The basic communication course at two- and four-year U.S. colleges and universities: Study VIII—The 40th anniversary. *Communication Education, 59*, 405–430. doi:10.1080/03634521003637124

Internet Sources

Aviv, R. (2007, November 4). Don't be shy. *The New York Times*. Retrieved from

http://www.nytimes.com/2007/11/04/education/edlife/reticence.html?pagewanted=all&_r=0

Citing Internet Sources

👤 Carefully select Internet or Web sources. Do not use Web documents from unknown authors or organizations. Personal Web materials are suspect, may not be reliable, and should not be used.

👤 Use Web materials that can be verified and compared to other sources. Research the author's background before using the information.

👤 Do not use an abridged version of a published source. Cite the complete printed source.

👤 Apply rules of documentation to Internet sources as well as traditionally published sources.

Informative Speech Sample Outline

Informative Speech
Speaker Name: _____

Thesis: Good or bad, all people experience stress and cope with it in various ways.

Introduction

I. The red lights flash.

II. Good or bad, all people experience stress and cope with it in various ways.

Body

I. Stress can be good or bad.
   A. Stress can be positive. (1)
   B. Stress can be negative. (2)

II. Stress affects the human body.
   A. There are symptoms of stress. (3)
   B. Chronic stress can affect your health. (4)

III. People cope with stress in various ways.
   A. People cope with stress in negative ways. (5) (6)
   B. People cope with stress in positive ways. (7)

Conclusion

I. Stress is a universal experience resulting in changes that people deal with using numerous techniques.

II. Good or bad, all people experience stress and cope with it in various ways.

References

Aldwin, C. M., Sutton, K., & Lachman, M. (1996, December). The development of coping resources in

   adulthood. *The Journal of Personality, 64* (4), 91–113. doi:10.1111/j.1467-6494.1996.tb00946.x

Brown, A. M. (2011, October 9). Family lifelines: Handling parenting stress. *The Pittsburg Morning Sun.*

   Retrieved from http://www.morningsun.net/news/x663895319/

   FAMILY-LIFELINES-Handling-parenting-stress

Harvard Medical School. (2011, September). Stress and overeating: Stress hormones increase appetites

   and a craving for high-fat, sugary food. *Harvard Health Letter, 36* (11), 6. Retrieved from

   http://www.health.harvard.edu/newsletters/harvard_health_letter/2011/September

Rula, H. (2011, September 28). Stress has real physical effects on the body. *East Valley Tribune.* Retrieved from

   http://www.eastvalleytribune.com/get_out/living_well/article_a3caf6bc-e86d-11e0-8428-001cc4c002e0.html

Smith, M., Segal, R., & Segal, J. (2011, October). *Understanding stress: Symptoms, signs, causes,*

   and effects. Retrieved from http://helpguide.org/mental/stress _signs.htm

Speaker Note Card

Introduction:
  Red
  Experience stress cope various
  Good (1)
  Affects human body (2)
  Symptoms (3)
  Chronic affect health (4)
  Cope
  Negative (5) (6) (7)

Conclusion:
  universal experience deal numerous techniques

Evidence Cards

1

Author: Anna Mae Brown

Date: October 9, 2011

Title: Family lifelines: Handling parenting stress

Publication: *The Pittsburg Morning Sun*

Positive stress is what gets us up and going every day. Some stress works positively for us by providing the extra energy to help us work through our problems or to react in sudden situations, such as when a deer suddenly jumps in front of our vehicle.

2

Author: Anna Mae Brown

Date: October 9, 2011

Title: Family lifelines: Handling parenting stress

Publication: *The Pittsburg Morning Sun*

But stress works negatively for us when it becomes too great for us to handle…
When we don't cope well, stress can cause us sickness, mental distress, and can affect our relations with others.

3

Author: Dr. Heidi Rula

Date: September 28, 2011

Title: Stress has real effects on the body

Publication: *East Valley Tribune*

Cortisol, often referred to as the "stress" hormone. Cortisol not only helps your body deal with stress in the flight-or-fight response… feel tired all the time, have decreased ability to handle stress and/or crave salty or sweet food.

Author: Smith, M., Segal, R., & Segal, J.   **4**

Date: October 2011

Title: Understanding stress: Symptoms, signs, causes, and effects

Publication: Helpguide.org

Chronic stress disrupts nearly every system in your body. It can raise blood pressure, suppress the immune system, increase the risk of heart attack and stroke, contribute to infertility, and speed up the aging process. Long-term stress can even rewire the brain, leaving you more vulnerable to anxiety and depression.

Author: Aldwin, C. M., Sutton, K., & Lachman, M.   **5**

Date: 1996

Title: The development of coping resources in adulthood

Publication: *The Journal of Personality*

Individuals often chose negative strategies to cope with stressful experiences, such as blaming others, escapism, or using drugs or alcohol to relieve the stress. These methods resulted in poorer outcomes.

Author: Harvard Medical School   **6**

Date: September 2011

Title: Stress and overeating: Stress hormones increase appetites and a craving for high-fat, sugary food

Publication: *Harvard Health Letter*

Stress hormones increase appetites and a craving for high-fat, sugary food.

Warhol, P., Ph.D., Psychiatrist   **7**

Date: October 5, 2011

Personal Interview
Individuals can use many approaches to coping with stress: remembering to breathe, exercise—at least 20 minutes a day, finding hobbies and a support system.

Checklist: Informative Speech

❑ Have you fulfilled the intent of the assignment—to inform?

❑ Has the instructor approved the topic?

❑ Does the subject of the speech conform to the assignment (object, place, animal, etc.)?

❑ Is the thesis a single declarative statement placed at the top of the outline and announced at the end of the introduction?

❑ Do you have five outside sources of information, of which three are from peer-reviewed sources?

❑ Have you prepared oral documentation from the outside sources?

❑ Is the outline in correct form, using complete sentences?

❑ Are you prepared to hand in two copies of the outline the day you speak?

❑ Do you have two copies of the reference section included on the outlines?

❑ Is the reference section alphabetized?

❑ Are speaker notes limited to 20 words on the speaker note card, with separate note cards for documentation of supporting materials?

❑ Have you rehearsed the speech within the four to six minute time limit?

❑ Have you prepared an introduction and a conclusion?

❑ Have you developed transitions to move from one point of the speech to another?

❑ Have you prepared an overview highlighting the main points?

❑ Is your delivery practice animated and fluent?

❑ Is eye contact direct and sustained?

❑ Do you have the checklist and the grading rubric ready to turn in?

Informative Speech Rubric

Speaker: _____   Grade (out of 100 points): _____

(Key: E = Excellent, G = Good, A = Average, F = Fair, P = Poor)

Outline & Note Cards

Followed the prescribed outline format	E G A F P
Used complete declarative sentences for each point on the outline	E G A F P
Used no more than 20 words on the outline note card	E G A F P
Followed the prescribed format for evidence note cards	E G A F P
Turned in two copies of the outline on the date of the speech	E G A F P
Turned in the completed checklist for this assignment	E G A F P

Invention

Tailored and adapted message to audience and the occasion	E G A F P
Achieved the general purpose of the assignment	E G A F P
Stayed within the prescribed assignment time limit	E G A F P
Developed a clear and concisely worded thesis statement	E G A F P
Achieved reasonably direct and communicative delivery	E G A F P
Used research resources to enhance supporting assertions	E G A F P
Orally documented all non-original material	E G A F P
Used at least three outside sources of information	E G A F P

Introduction

Grabbed attention of audience with unique, attention-getting device	E G A F P
Provided an obvious thesis statement	E G A F P
Previewed main points	E G A F P

Body

Included two, three, or four main points in the body of the speech	E G A F P
Supported each main point by at least two subordinate points	E G A F P
Supported subordinate points with evidence from research resources	E G A F P
Presented main points in a specific order	E G A F P
Made main points have focus and connection to the thesis	E G A F P
Regularly used transitions between the main points	E G A F P

Conclusion

Clearly summarized main point	E G A F P
Restated the thesis	E G A F P
Included no new information	E G A F P

Style

Used acceptable grammar, pronunciation, and clear articulation	E G A F P
Demonstrated an understanding of accuracy, clarity, appropriateness, and vividness in language use	E G A F P

Delivery

Maintained sustained eye contact with the audience	E G A F P
Stayed composed and resisted distractions	E G A F P
Recited speech extemporaneously	E G A F P
Had vocal variety	E G A F P
Had appropriate volume	E G A F P
Used the body as a communicative instrument	E G A F P

General Comments

Speech Assignment 3: Indictment Speech

The indictment speech assignment begins the ultimate thrust of the course. This speech is intended to maximize your ability to do research on a critical issue and apply that research to verbal advocacy in changing the status quo.

Basically, you must (a) research an issue to determine whether a problem exists with the status quo; (b) formulate a proposition of policy that would lead to a change in those conditions; and (c) develop a speech that proves, using evidence and reasoning, that a problems truly does exist—hence justifying the thesis.

The overriding assumption of this assignment is that one must not indict a system or condition without proving that actual harm results from that system. Therefore, it is assumed that you will construct the statements of harm carefully based on the best and most applicable evidence. The reasoning from the evidence should reveal carefully thought-out main points (indictments) and subpoints.

Perhaps the most common error at this juncture is the tendency to draw hasty generalizations about the existence of problems, when little evidence warrants those conclusions. That error and other logical fallacies can be avoided by careful research and by constantly testing the conclusions drawn from the research.

Although this assignment is primarily one of logical proof, other rhetorical aspects must be kept in mind (see Speech Assignment 5: Speech Criticism). Specifically, your task is to:

1. Construct an enforceable proposition of policy that changes the status quo. This is the thesis sentence for the indictment and propositional speeches.

2. Construct two indictments of a present policy system that justify your proposition. These will be the main points of your speech.

3. Detail each indictment. Subpoints are required and must support the indictment.

4. On the left margin of the outline, construct a technical plot for each indictment.

5. Limit notes to 35 words (original) plus evidence cards.

6. Place the complete reference list on the back of each outline.

7. Be prepared to turn in three copies of the outline. You must have at least seven sources of information, three of which must be peer reviewed.

8. Include an introduction and a conclusion.

9. Practice the speech within a total time limit of five to seven minutes.

10. Clear your proposition and indictments with your instructor.

11. Because this is primarily an assignment in logical proof, apply all rules of evidence and reasoning.

Note: An additional speech on this proposition will be given later.

Sample Propositions of Policy

The federal government should raise the minimum wage to $12.00 an hour.

The Food and Drug Administration should adopt stricter regulations regarding pharmacy compounding.

The State of South Dakota should enact a comprehensive program for funding higher education.

Indictment Speech Sample Outline

Indictment Speech
Speaker Name: _____

Proposition

OSHA (the Occupational Health and Safety Administration) should establish a policy that prohibits the use of personal cell phones in medical workplaces.

Introduction

    I. When we go to the doctor, we expect our experiences to be private.

    II. OSHA (the Occupational Health and Safety Administration) should establish a policy that prohibits the use of personal cell phones in medical workplaces.

Body

Technical Plot

Indictment	I.	Texting is disrespectful and wasteful to health-care companies.
Example		A. Personal cell phone use causes disrespectful customer service in medical workplaces. (1)
Testimony		B. Texting during work time wastes health-care dollars. (2) (3)
Indictment	II.	The use of cell phones threatens privacy and safety of medical service.
Example		A. Camera photos violate patient privacy. (4) (5) (6)
Testimony		B. Cell phone use threatens patient safety. (7) (8) (9) (10)

Conclusion

    I. The use of cell phones is disrespectful, wasteful, threatens privacy, safety, and accuracy of health-care service.

    II. OSHA (the Occupational Health and Safety Administration) should establish a policy that prohibits the use of personal cell phones in medical workplaces.

References

Chester, E. (2012). *Reviving Work Ethic: A Leader's Guide to Ending Entitlement and Restoring Pride in the Emerging Workforce.* Austin, TX: Greenleaf Book Group Press.

Frings, C. S. (2006, April). Addressing management issues. *Medical Laboratory Observer, 38* (4), 28–29. Retrieved from EBSCOhost.

Hans, N., & Kapadia, F. N. (2008, October). Effects of mobile phone use on specific intensive care unit devices. *Indian Journal of Critical Care Medicine, 12* (4), 170–173.

Jeske, H. C., Tiefenthaler, W., Hohlrieder, M., et al. (2007). Bacterial contamination of anesthetists' hands by personal mobile phone and fixed phone use in the operating theater. *Anesthesia, 62,* 904–906.

Shepherd, A. (2010, June 7). Negative exposure. *For the Record, 22* (11), 10. Retrieved from http://www.fortherecordmag.com/archives/060710p10.shtml

Speaker Note Card

Introduction

     I. Visit doctor ➡ private.

     II. OSHA (Occupational Health & Safety Administration) should establish …policy that prohibits …use …personal cell phones… medical workplaces.

          I.

               A.   disrespectful customer service

               B.   wastes dollars

          II.

               A.   photos violates privacy

               B.   phone threatens safety

Conclusion

     I. Review

     II. Thesis

Evidence Cards

1

Author: C. S. Frings
Date: April 2006
Title: Addressing management issues
Publication: *Medical Laboratory Observer*

Frings tells the story of an assistant lab manager whose staff members are frequently busy on their cell phones, thus unable to provide service to fellow health-care professionals or customers.

2

Author: C. S. Frings
Date: April 2006
Title: Addressing management issues
Publication: *Medical Laboratory Observer*

Unless a cell phone is being used by a staff member for work itself, personal cell phone use on the job is disruptive … and robs an employer of productive time.

3

Author: Eric Chester
Date: 2012
Title: *Reviving Work Ethic: A Leader's Guide to Ending Entitlement and Restoring Pride in the Emerging Workplace*

One general manager lamented that... texting had become a major distraction for her young employees and was hurting the bottom line.

4

Author: A. Shepherd
Date: June 7, 2010
Title: Negative Exposure
Publication: *For the record*

"several employees and other individuals at Florida's Martin Memorial Health Systems allegedly used their cell phone cameras in the emergency department to photograph the injuries of a shark attack victim who later died."

5

Author: A. Shepherd
Date: June 7, 2010
Title: Negative exposure
Publication: *For the Record*

In February 2009, Mercy Walworth Medical Center in Lake Geneva, Wis., dismissed two nurses for allegedly using their cell phone cameras to take photos of a patient's X-ray and later posting them on the Internet.

6

Author: A. Shepherd
Date3: June 7, 2010
Title: Negative exposure
Publication: *For the Record*

"The risk of privacy violations and consequent harm has increased tremendously with the proliferation of devices such as cell phone cameras and audio recorders because it's so easy to upload pictures and audio files from cell phones to the Internet," says Patricia Markus, JD.

7

Author: C. S. Frings
Date: April 2006
Title: Addressing management issues
Publication: *Medical Laboratory Observer*

With the huge stream of information being captured and reported from the laboratory, talking on the cell phone while working adds an unnecessary risk to quality… You must keep cell phones put away due to potential biohazard contamination of the phone in the work area.

8

Authors: H. C. Jeske, et al.
Date: 2007
Title: Bacterial contamination of anesthetists' hands by personal mobile phone and fixed phone use in the operating theater.
Publication: *Anesthesia*

From cell phone use, "38 of 40 anesthetist providers working in the OR had bacterial contamination on their hands after first disinfecting their hands."

9

Author: C. S. Frings
Date: April 2006
Title: Addressing management issues
Publication: *Medical Laboratory Observer*

There are hospitals that have restrictions on cell phones due to interference with pacemakers.

10

Authors: Hans & Kapadia
Date: October 2008
Title: Effects of mobile phone use on specific intensive care unit devices.
Publication: *Indian Journal of Critical Care Medicine*
               Pages 170–173.

Mobile phones have an adverse effect on the medical devices used in critical care setup.

Checklist: Indictment Speech

❑ Have the proposition and indictments been approved by your instructor?

❑ Is the thesis statement (proposition) an enforceable proposition of policy that advocates a change in the status quo?

❑ Does the proposition cite a mandating agency and include the word *should*?

❑ Does the speech include two indictments (main points) stating harm?

❑ Have you developed subpoints to support each indictment?

❑ Have you included a technical plot?

❑ Is the outline in proper form with a developed introduction and conclusion?

❑ Are you prepared to turn in three copies of the outline on the day of the speech?

❑ Do the outlines contain the reference section?

❑ Do you have seven sources of information?

❑ Does the speaker note card contain 35 (or fewer) words?

❑ Have you prepared source cards for documentation?

❑ Is the speech five to seven minutes in length?

❑ Is the speech fluent, with good eye contact, transitions, and overviews?

❑ Are you prepared to hand in the checklist and the grading rubric on the day of your speech?

Indictment Speech Rubric

Speaker: _____ Grade (out of 100 points): _____

(Key: E = Excellent, G = Good, A = Average, F = Fair, P = Poor)

Outline & Note Cards

Followed the prescribed outline format   E G A F P

Used complete declarative sentences for each point on the outline   E G A F P

Used no more than 35 words on the outline note card   E G A F P

Followed the prescribed format for evidence note cards   E G A F P

Turned in two copies of the outline on the date of the speech   E G A F P

Turned in the completed assignment checklist for this assignment   E G A F P

Included a technical plot on the outline   E G A F P

Invention

Tailored and adapted message to audience and the occasion   E G A F P

Achieved the general purpose of the assignment   E G A F P

Stayed within the prescribed assignment time limit   E G A F P

Developed a clear and concisely worded thesis statement   E G A F P

Achieved reasonably direct and communicative delivery   E G A F P

Used research resources to enhance supporting assertions   E G A F P

Orally documented all non-original material   E G A F P

Used at least three outside sources of information   E G A F P

Applied all rules and effectively employed reasoning   E G A F P

Introduction

Grabbed attention of audience with unique, attention-getting device   E G A F P

Provided an obvious thesis statement   E G A F P

Previewed main points   E G A F P

Body

Included two indictments in the body of the speech   E G A F P

Supported each main point by at least two subordinate points   E G A F P

Supported subordinate points with evidence from research resources   E G A F P

Presented main points in a specific order   E G A F P

Made main points have focus and connection to the thesis   E G A F P

Regularly used transitions between the main points   E G A F P

Conclusion

Clearly summarized main point   E G A F P

Restated the thesis   E G A F P

Included no new information   E G A F P

Style

Used acceptable grammar, pronunciation, and clear articulation   E G A F P

Demonstrated an understanding of accuracy, clarity, appropriateness, and vividness in language use   E G A F P

Delivery

Maintained eye contact with the audience   E G A F P

Stayed composed and resisted distractions   E G A F P

Recited speech extemporaneously   E G A F P

Had vocal variety   E G A F P

Had appropriate volume   E G A F P

Used the body as a communicative instrument   E G A F P

General Comments

_____

_____

_____

Speech Assignment 4: Propositional Speech

The propositional speech is the culmination of your individual effort to convince an audience to accept your policy thesis. Often, people end their public speaking with an indictment of a system. Sound rhetorical practice, however, generally goes one step further—presenting a responsible solution to the problem you have proven exists.

As dictated by the assignment, more than half of your communication time will be spent delineating a plan of action to be implemented and explaining how that plan will work best in a practical setting. Specifically, you should:

1. Develop the total speech to convince the audience of the proposition chosen for your indictment speech.

2. Construct the speech to consist of
   a. the two indictments you used in your previous speech,
   b. a plan of action that will implement your proposition,
   c. a section justifying your solution.

3. Make the speech six to eight minutes long.

4. Include on your note card 45 words (original) plus evidence cards for supporting material.

5. Use the required outline format (on the following pages).

6. Include with each outline a reference section specific to this speech. Two copies of the outline are required.

7. Use sources not used in the indictment speech if you wish. A specific number of sources is not required.

8. Do not use a technical plot.

Propositional Speech Sample Outline

Prepositional Speech

Speaker Name: _____

Thesis: The Department of Veterans Affairs should initiate mandatory counseling sessions for all servicemen and -women.

Introduction

I. Suicide has become a reality to our families and our communities, but also our United States veterans.

II. The Department of Veterans Affairs should initiate mandatory counseling sessions for all servicemen and -women.

Body

I. The suicide rate among servicemen and -women is increasing.
   A. More soldiers are dying from suicide than from combat. (1)
   B. Soldiers are going on multiple combat tours. (2)

II. It is not always easy for soldiers to receive psychological help.
   A. Soldiers face a different world when they return home, and they do not know what to do. (3)
   B. There are not enough resources available to provide service to soldiers in need of mental health care. (4)

III. Every soldier should be required to attend mental health counseling after returning home from a combat tour.
   A. The costs of providing mental healthcare for our veterans will be funded by the Department of Veterans Affairs. (5)
   B. Each counselor will be required to have the specific skills it takes to counsel a veteran, especially one with post-traumatic stress disorder (PTSD). (6)

IV. This plan will work for a number of reasons.
   A. PTSD is best treated through multi-method treatment. (7)
   B. Many people fear appearing weak and asking for help. (8)

Conclusion

I. Our soldiers are fighting for us, so we need to give back and fight for them.

II. The Department of Veterans Affairs should initiate mandatory counseling sessions for all servicemen and -women.

References

Clifton, E. (2010, January 13). Suicide rate surged among veterans. *IPS - Inter Press Service*.

Retrieved from http://ipsnews.net/news.asp?idnews=49971

Hazo, S. (2008, June). The time it takes to see. *Vital Speeches of the Day*, 74 (6). PTSD Recovery. (2010).

Morningside Recovery. Retrieved from http://morningsiderecovery.com/mental-illness/ptsd

Reickoff, P. (2010, August 2). Why the suicide rate among veterans is increasing [Video file].

Retrieved from http://bigthink.com/ideas/22859. *Veterans: After VA survey shows long wait times for*

mental health care, chairman Murray calls for action. (2011). Lanham, MD: Federal Information &

News Dispatch, Inc.

Zivin, K., Kim, M. H., McCarthy, J. F., Austin, K. L., Hoggatt, K. J., Walters, H., & Valenstein, M. (2007).

Suicide mortality among individuals receiving treatment for depression in the Veterans Affairs health

system. *American Journal of Public Health*, 97 (12), 2193–2198.

Checklist: Propositional Speech

❑ Does the speech fulfill the assignment—a total speech to persuade?

❑ Does the speech include a review of the indictments from the previous speech?

❑ Did you include a plan of action?

❑ Have you included a justification of the solution?

❑ Have you addressed the issues of enforcement and financing?

❑ Have you addressed the issue of desirability?

❑ Are speaker notes limited to 45 words on the outline card, with evidence cards for supporting material?

❑ Does the outline adhere to the required format?

❑ Have you developed a specific reference section for this speech?

❑ Have you made two copies of the outline for the instructor?

❑ Have you included two copies of the reference section with the outline?

❑ Have you developed transitions and an overview?

❑ When you practice does the speech fall into the time range of six to eight minutes?

❑ Do you have the checklist and grading rubric ready to hand in on the day you speak?

❑ Has your rehearsal prepared you for optimum delivery—eye contact, fluency, etc.?

❑ Is the delivery focused for a persuasive, conversational presentation?

Propositional Speech Rubric

Speaker: _____ Grade (out of 100 points): _____

(Key: E = Excellent, G = Good, A = Average, F = Fair, P = Poor)

Outline & Note Cards

Followed the prescribed outline format	E G A F P
Used complete declarative sentences for each point on the outline	E G A F P
Used no more than 45 words on the outline note card	E G A F P
Followed the prescribed format for evidence note cards	E G A F P
Turned in two copies of the outline on the date of the speech	E G A F P
Turned in the completed assignment checklist for this assignment	E G A F P

Invention

Tailored and adapted message to audience and the occasion	E G A F P
Achieved the general purpose of the assignment	E G A F P
Stayed within the prescribed assignment time limit	E G A F P
Developed a clear and concisely worded thesis statement	E G A F P
Achieved reasonably direct and communicative delivery	E G A F P
Used research resources to enhance supporting assertions	E G A F P
Orally documented all non-original material	E G A F P
Used at least three outside sources of information	E G A F P
Applied all rules and effectively employed reasoning	E G A F P

Introduction

Grabbed attention of audience with unique, attention-getting device	E G A F P
Provided an obvious thesis statement	E G A F P
Previewed main points	E G A F P

Body

Included two indictments, a plan, and justification of the plan in the body of the speech	E G A F P
Supported each main point by at least two subordinate points	E G A F P
Supported subordinate points with evidence from research resources	E G A F P
Presented main points in a specific order	E G A F P
Made main points have focus and connection to the thesis	E G A F P
Regularly used transitions between the main points	E G A F P

Conclusion

Clearly summarized main point	E G A F P
Restated the thesis	E G A F P
Included no new information	E G A F P

Style

Used acceptable grammar, pronunciation, and clear articulation	E G A F P
Demonstrated an understanding of accuracy, clarity, appropriateness, and vividness in language use	E G A F P

Delivery

Maintained sustained eye contact with the audience	E G A F P
Stayed composed and resisted distractions	E G A F P
Recited speech extemporaneously	E G A F P
Had vocal variety	E G A F P
Had appropriate volume	E G A F P
Used the body as a communicative instrument	E G A F P

General Comments

_____

_____

_____

Speech Assignment 5: Speech Criticism

This assignment is designed to accomplish the course objectives through criticism. Criticism is using our abilities to clarify our reactions, to gather specific instances to support our reasons, and to suggest ways in which we might improve our presentation.

We are all involved in criticism. We criticize movies, TV programs, food, books, class lectures. Not all of our criticism is designed to help the individual or the event being criticized. The art of criticism often is abused and overused. As we use the term here, criticism means evaluation.

Some of the benefits of this assignment are to see yourself as your peers do. The feedback you receive should strengthen or weaken previous self-criticism of your speeches. It also should help you speak in the future. Further, because you most likely will be approached through speech to accept another's ideas or products, it should help you make rational judgments of others' persuasive ideas.

Although all interpretation of criticism is arbitrary, you are expected to follow an established standard of criticism. The emphasis on standards is changing constantly because society is continually changing, and the socially oriented critic reflects a standard that is related closely to what is needed at a given time.

When planning the listening phase of this assignment, keep in mind that you are moving from the role of self-critic to that of critic of your peers' speeches.

Assignment requirements are as follows.

1. Write one speech criticism based on the indictment speech.

2. Adhere to a minimum length of 600 words.

3. Hand in two copies of the criticism to the instructor when due.

4. Turn in the copy in standard type, single spaced, and double spaced between paragraphs.

5. Use a topical organization based on the four canons of rhetoric and the outline/essay form. Underline topic headings, and write paragraphs responding to the question.

6. Make criticism specific.

7. Evaluate, don't summarize, what was said.

8. Use as many examples from the speech as possible.

9. Include a title page with your name, date, section number, and the name of the speaker evaluated. Place the name of the speaker at the top of each page of his/her evaluation.

10. Turn in criticisms one week after the speech. No late papers are accepted. Also hand in the Speech Criticism grading rubric when you turn in the criticism.

11. Get a copy of the speaker's outline on the day he or she speaks.

12. Use the following speech criticism criteria.

Speech Criticism Criteria

I. Invention: The speaker's resources and their influence on an audience

    A. *Research resources:*

        1. Was it evident that the speaker had researched the subject carefully? Why or why not? That is:

            a. Did the speaker use carefully documented supporting materials that indicated depth of research? Did you check the bibliography at the library? What did you find?

            b. Could the speaker successfully answer questions posed following the speech? Give specific examples to support your opinion.

    B. *Three methods of influencing an audience:*

        1. Ethical proof:

            a. Intelligence. In your opinion, did the speaker know what he/she was talking about? Why or why not?

            b. Good will and/or character. In your opinion, was the speaker really interested in informing you about a vital topic? What gave you that impression?

        2. Emotional proof:

            a. Do you think you had a need for this information? Why or why not?

            b. Was your curiosity about the subject aroused? Why or why not?

            c. In general, did the speaker try to adapt the speech to your interests? If so, how did he/she adapt? If not, why not? Give specific examples.

        3. Logical proof:

            a. Evidence. Was the evidence plentiful? Was it well documented? Was it related verbally back to the point under consideration?

            b. Reasoning. Did the evidence the speaker used really support what he/she was saying? That is, did the indictments the speaker made actually stem from the evidence, or not? Give examples of the success or failure to do this. What reasoning patterns did the speaker use?

II. Arrangement: Organization of the speaker's ideas

    A. *Introduction:*

        1. Did the introduction capture your attention? Why or why not?

        2. Did it give a background of the subject?

        3. Did it indicate what direction the speech would take?

        4. Was the thesis stated clearly at the end of the introduction?

        5. Was there anything else significant about the introduction? (Be sure to give examples from the speech to support your answers to the above.)

    B. *Body:*

        1. What type of organizational pattern was used? Was it the best choice for the speech? Why?

        2. Were the main points clearly stated? Were they repeated often?

        3. Did the supporting points directly relate to or explain the main points? Why or why not? Were they clearly stated? Repeated?

4. Were the transitions between main points clear and smooth? If not, what might be done to improve them?

5. Do you think the audience (without an outline) could easily follow this speech? Why or why not?

C. *Conclusion:*

1. Did the conclusion summarize the major points and thesis of the speech?

2. Did it include new information? (It should not!)

3. Did the speaker seem to have trouble concluding?

4. Were there any other strong or weak points? Give examples.

III. Style: Using language to convey ideas

1. Was the speaker's language clear? Did he/she define technical terms?

2. Did the speaker explain each point concisely, or was there excess verbiage? Give examples.

3. Was the language appropriate for this audience? Why or why not?

4. Were there any particularly vivid supporting materials? Give examples.

5. Did the speaker use correct grammar?

IV. Delivery: Skills in actually presenting the completed speech

1. Was the speaker's eye contact direct and sustained? Did the speaker's use of note cards help or hinder eye contact? Did he/she read note cards excessively rather than using them to aid communication?

2. Was the delivery conversational or was it memorized? Why do you think so?

3. Did the speaker exhibit symptoms of stage fright, or was he/she poised? What would you suggest to improve his/her poise?

4. How enthusiastic was the speaker's delivery? Did he/she seem bored with the subject? If so, how did this attitude affect you as a listener?

Speech Criticism

Good Computer Hackers Are Necessary

Speech by: _____

Critic:

Date: 10/19/2012

SPCM 101

Section #1

I. Invention

A. Research resources

Kayla did a really nice job with her research. Each resource came from either an online database or an online version of a magazine, both of which are credible sources. Not only were her sources credible but all but one of them are from the past two years, thus fulfilling the "current" component of the 3 C's of research. It seemed that her resources must also have been quite comprehensive, because when Kayla was questioned about regulation at the end of her speech, she responded with authority and fluidity, so she was obviously well versed in the subject matter. Kayla offered advice regarding how officials regulate and test "good" computer hackers so that they are more trusted and easily distinguished from "bad" computer hackers.

B. Methods of influencing an audience

1. Ethical proof

Kayla was obviously well informed about her topic because of the fluidity of the speech and the ease with which she answered my question. Her research was solid, and I could tell that she had a personal interest in the story, which kept the audience and myself interested. The only thing I felt was lacking in the area of ethos was the reason she was interested in the topic, or why the topic relates to her. True, she related the topic of computer use to the audience by listing the many uses that we have for computers, but I would have liked a more personal connection. Based on what I know about Kayla from her previous two speeches, the topic of computer hacking seems slightly random, so I was lost as to why she chose such a topic. Nevertheless, I could tell that she was interested, and I did not find my mind wandering away from the speech.

2. Emotional proof

The audience did have a need for this information because we are all college students, and we use computer technology daily. Kayla began her speech by declaring a few of the most common uses of computers, such as for research or for playing video games. I would have liked to see a stronger connection between the idea of being in college and the idea of computer use. There was definitely a brief reference at the beginning of the speech, but I feel that the two ideas are so easily related that Kayla should have made a more specific connection to the audience. For example, she could have used an example of the computer resources at South Dakota State University or a report of any past cases of hacking at this university. Both of these would have been more specific ways to connect the content with the audience. However, my curiosity for the subject was aroused because I had never thought of any benefits from the concept of computer hacking, which is generally thought of in a negative light. I enjoyed hearing about the subject from this new perspective.

3. Logical proof

Kayla's evidence was both plentiful and well documented. She incorporated definition, personal example, other examples, and statistics into her speech. She did a decent job of orally documenting her resources, and she included all necessary elements in that documentation. However, when referencing a source that has already been documented, Kayla should not repeat the entire oral documentation, but rather simply refer to the previous source. The repetition of the entire documentation quickly became tedious. On the references page, there were a few mistakes with the inclusion of unnecessary information and the lack of an author on the *Computer Hacking* source. In her speech, each source was easily related to the topic at hand. Kayla used generalization as her reasoning pattern by providing several examples of the negative effects of computer hacking. This generalization shows the problem at hand and displays a reason for change. The examples and statistics used in the speech did a good job of supporting Kayla's main point. One personal example was of a friend whose college fund was hacked, thus leaving her without money saved for college. This provided a clear example of the dangers of hackers.

II. Arrangement

A. Introduction

The introduction to the speech caught my attention with a definition of the word *hacking*. This provided a basis for what would be talked about for the remainder of the presentation. However, the exact words said as the first sentence of the speech were different than those printed on the speech outline. Next, Kayla provided some background for the subject both by defining the word and by explaining some of the common uses of computers. As mentioned before, she could have done a better job of specifically relating these uses to the audience full of SDSU students. Another piece of background information that should have been presented is what constitutes a "good" hacker versus a "bad" hacker, because I was left wondering this throughout the speech. At the end of the introduction, the thesis was stated very clearly, and Kayla previewed the rest of the speech.

B. Body

This speech demonstrated a topical organization pattern, which is very appropriate for an indictment speech. The main points are the two topics, so the speech flows from one to the other in a topical pattern. The main points were clearly stated in the thesis and conclusion, but they could have been presented more clearly and repeated more often in the body paragraphs. Similarly, the subpoints could be stated more often just to increase clarity. Because I had the speech outline in front of me, I was able to follow along, but I believe without the outline the audience may have heard a blend from the introduction into the main points. This blending could have been avoided with the use of better transitions. The introduction set up a great preview, but after that there was little audible transitioning from point to point. The use of review-preview would have been helpful to clarify the distinctions between points. That being said, the transition into the conclusion was very strong and very obvious because of both audible and physical cues. Kayla began with "In conclusion…," which is simple yet effective, and she took a more powerful physical stance. With regard to main points and subpoints, the latter definitely supported the former. Kayla's evidence supported the subpoints, which related to the main points, which supported the thesis. This was very clear both on paper and in the speech. The evidence and subpoints were effective because they directly related to the main ideas.

C. Conclusion

The conclusion was very brief, but it was strong. Kayla reiterated the two main points clearly and then proceeded to restate her thesis from the introduction. She did not incorporate any new information or bring up any new ideas. She had no trouble concluding, and I believe that the brevity of the conclusion served well as a quick way to sum up the speech. As mentioned before, the transition into the conclusion was very strong because Kayla showed both a physical cue that she was beginning the conclusion and a verbal statement of conclusion.

III. Style

The language that Kayla employed in her speech was both clear and appropriate for the audience. She gave a clear definition of the word *hacker* so that the audience was all on the same page, and then the rest of the language was all easy to understand because the terminology used was not too technical. She explained each point well and allowed her examples to provide evidence for each subpoint. She included the example of a friend whose college savings account was hacked, resulting in the loss of all the money in the fund. This example was particularly emotive to the audience, because we are all paying for college, so it is hard to imagine losing an entire fund to a problematic hacker. Kayla spoke very clearly and with correct grammar; there were no instances in which I was confused about what she was saying. The only excess verbiage in the speech was the repetition of the oral citations and the words *like* and *um*. Obviously, these are common filler words that should be eliminated. I can tell that the only times Kayla uses these words are when she is struggling to phrase the words she intends to say relating to the topic. Next time, if this problem still exists, it may be better to leave a silent pause rather than fill the space with filler words such as these.

IV. Delivery

Throughout her speech, Kayla maintained great eye contact. She looked down at her note cards only a few times for reference and also to read through her evidence. This definitely did not hinder her performance because even though she was reading evidence off of the cards, it was obvious that she had practiced and prepared, so the speech ran smoothly. Because of her obvious preparation, the speech remained conversational. Kayla did not appear to be experiencing any extreme nervousness other than the good adrenaline that typically runs through your veins when beginning a speech. She began the introduction with confidence and remained poised throughout the rest of the presentation. The only suggestion I have for her is to have a little more inflection in her voice so that the vocal range can expand. While this did not distract from this speech, it is a good challenge for the next one. Kayla obviously cares about the issue and definitely did not seem bored with the subject. Her speech left me wondering about the benefits of "good" computer hacking and the means of regulation to employ such hackers without risk of confusion with "bad" hackers.

Speech Criticism Rubric

	Excellent	Good	Needs Improvement	Points Awarded
Invention (20 Points)	Addressed all of the criticism criteria for this section. Included specific examples from the speech delivery to illustrate your opinion.	Most of the criticism criteria were addressed for this section. A limited number of specific examples from the speech delivery were used to illustrate your opinion.	This section provided little or no details on the speaker's use of invention. More detail and specific examples are needed to support your analysis.	
Arrangement (20 Points)	Addressed all of the criticism criteria for this section. Included specific examples from the speech delivery to illustrate your opinion.	Most of the criticism criteria were addressed for this section. A limited number of specific examples from the speech delivery were used to illustrate your opinion.	This section provided little or no details on the speaker's use of arrangement. More detail and specific examples are needed to support your analysis.	
Style (20 Points)	Addressed all of the criticism criteria for this section. Included specific examples from the speech delivery to illustrate your opinion.	Most of the criticism criteria were addressed for this section. A limited number of specific examples from the speech delivery were used to illustrate your opinion.	This section provided little or no details on the speaker's use of style. More detail and specific examples are needed to support your analysis.	
Delivery (20 Points)	Addressed all of the criticism criteria for this section. Included specific examples from the speech delivery to illustrate your opinion.	Most of the criticism criteria were addressed for this section. A limited number of specific examples from the speech delivery were used to illustrate your opinion.	This section provided little or no details on the speaker's use of delivery. More detail and specific examples are needed to support your analysis.	
Grammatical Structure (10 Points)	The analysis was free of grammatical and spelling errors.	The analysis contained minimal grammatical and spelling errors.	The analysis contained several grammatical and spelling errors, which made reading the paper difficult.	
Requirements (10 Points)	The criticism was typewritten, single spaced, and contained a title page. In addition, two copies of the criticism were turned in.	Some of the basic assignment requirements were not met.	You failed to meet the basic assignment requirements.	

Comments:

_____

_____

_____

Total: _____

Speech Assignment 6: Group Discussion

Your group assignment is to solve a contemporary problem collectively in a panel discussion format. History has indicated that when significant problems are beyond the scope of the individual communicator, people have banded together to solve problems. Often, through verbal cooperation among individuals, seemingly unsolvable problems have been put into proper perspective and dealt with satisfactorily.

This is not to say that facets of a problem automatically can be agreed upon, let alone their solution(s). Indeed, bringing people together in a crisis or simulated crisis situation often provokes a certain amount of ill will. Nevertheless, once the maxim is accepted that "it is better to discuss a problem without resolving it than to resolve a problem without discussing it," communicative cooperation toward a designed goal may begin.

Specifically, your task is as follows:

1. Divide into discussion groups.
2. Choose a group leader.
3. Select a topic.
4. Choose a suitable discussion question.
5. Individually research all aspects of the question.
6. Construct individual discussion outlines, and then collectively construct a group outline. The outlines are to be in question form and follow the progression prescribed.
7. Present the panel discussion.

Sample Discussion Questions

1. To what extent, if any, should the federal government provide economic aid for urban revitalization?
2. What should be U.S. policy regarding campaign financing?
3. What, if anything, should be done to further protect wetlands?

Group members' names:

Discussion Progression

    I. What initial explanations are necessary?

       A. What terms in the question should be defined?

       B. What, if any, limitations should be imposed on the question?

    II. What facts are important in an analysis of the question? (Indictments) What *harmful effects* are present that deserve attention? (Harmful effects prove a problem.)

       A.

          1. ?

          2. ?

          3. ?

       B.

          1. ?

          2. ?

          3. ?

    III. What are the causes of the problem?

    IV. What is the best solution?

    V. How can this solution be implemented?

(**Note:** III, IV, and V are not on the group outline, although there may be time for them to be included in the class discussion.)

Note: This discussion progression is modeled after the reflective thinking sequence of John Dewey.

Group Discussion Sample Outline

Panel member's names:

Question: What, if anything, should be done in regard to adolescents and technology?

   I. What terms in the question should be defined?

      A. What terms, if any, in the question should be defined?

          1. What is an adolescent?

          2. What is technology?

          3. Other terms?

      B. Are any limitations imposed on the question?

          1. Any age limitations?

          2. Any specific technology limitations?

  II. What facts are important in an analysis of the question?

      A. What harmful effects, if any, are present?

          1. What are the educational harms?

          2. What are the social harms?

          3. What are the moral harms?

          4. What are the physical harms?

          5. What are the psychological harms?

          6. What are the financial harms?

          7. What are the political harms?

      B. What are the causes of the harms?

          1. What are the causes of the educational harms?

          2. What are the causes of the social harms?

          3. What are the causes of the moral harms?

          4. What are the causes of the physical harms?

          5. What are the causes of the psychological harms?

          6. What are the causes of the financial harms?

          7. What are the causes of the political harms?

Checklist: Discussion Assignment

❑ Has the discussion group chosen a group leader?

❑ Have all members of the group exchanged phone numbers and schedules?

❑ Has a suitable topic been chosen for the assignment?

❑ Has the topic been placed in question form?

❑ Has each member individually researched all aspects of the topic?

❑ Have individual outlines based on research been developed?

❑ Has a collective group outline been made?

❑ Do all members have a copy of the group outline?

❑ Has a copy of the group outline been prepared for the instructor?

❑ Is the outline in question format?

❑ Have all members contributed to the preparation and presentation of the discussion?

❑ Are group members prepared to document from supporting materials as well as offer personal opinions and ideas?

❑ Has the group prepared to interact and listen in a spontaneous and supportive way?

❑ Is each group member prepared to hand in the Group Discussion Speech rubric on the day of the presentation?

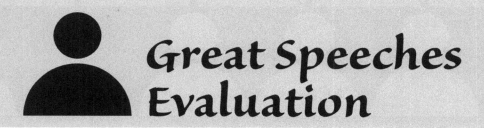

Great Speeches Evaluation

Name _____   Section Number _____

Videos

1. Ronald Reagan—Address on the Challenger Disaster
2. Martin Luther King, Jr.—I Have a Dream
3. Robert F. Kennedy—Remarks on the Assassination of Martin Luther King, Jr.

Key reasons for examining these speeches:

1. CONTEXT—Sometimes called SETTING
   - Specifically looking at the circumstances of the event and the audience analysis.
   - Context shapes the message and should influence the extent to which a speech is viewed as effective.
2. USE OF LANGUAGE
   - Specifically looking at vivid and dramatic language.
   - How does the speaker create a full mental picture?
3. DELIVERY
   - Use of voice, enthusiasm, eye contact, and gestures.

The Speeches

(Please list specific examples from the speeches in the space provided)

Reagan — "The Great Communicator"

USE OF LANGUAGE:

_____

_____

_____

_____

How was the delivery affected by the medium of television?

_____

_____

_____

_____

King — *Perhaps the most effective and beautiful speech ever delivered*

VOICE: (pay particular attention to phrasing, pacing, and inflections)

_____

_____

_____

_____

_____

LANGUAGE: (Vividness, metaphors, repetition, and parallelism)

_____

_____

_____

_____

_____

Kennedy — *One of the most effective eulogies ever delivered*

Please list specific examples in which the theme of justice is discussed.

_____

_____

_____

_____

_____

Kennedy had little time to prepare for this speech. Identify and list examples that gave the audience the impression that the speech was extemporaneous.

_____

_____

_____

_____

_____

Information Sheet

Name: _____ Phone: _____

Campus Address: _____

E-mail Address: _____

Age: _____ Year and Semester in College: _____

Major: _____ Minor: _____

Employer (if applicable): _____ Hours worked: _____

Hometown and high school attended: _____

Newspapers/magazines you read frequently: _____

_____

Books you read in the past year: _____

_____

_____

TV shows you watch frequently: _____

_____

_____

Activities and Interests:

_____

_____

_____

What previous courses in speech at the high school or college level have you taken?

_____

_____

_____

What previous experience of any type have you had involving an audience?

_____

_____

_____

What problems, if any, do you have with public speaking? Why?

_____

_____

_____

What do you hope to gain from this course?

_____

_____

_____

Glossary

Alternative causality The strategy of offering reasons that differ. (*See also* Causation)

Analogy Comparison of the known to the unknown.

Arrangement The canon of rhetoric that deals with the structure of the speech.

Articulation The clarity of speech sounds.

Attending Paying attention to, and focusing on, a speaker's message.

Audience The collection of individuals who are exposed to a speech.

Audience analysis A review of information about the audience, which is used to enhance speech preparation.

Authority Reasoning from the expert opinion of others.

Brainstorming A technique for generating a great number of ideas in which judgments are withheld for later evaluation.

Canon of rhetoric Guidelines or principles that guide the practice of public speaking.

Causation (or causal reasoning) Reasoning that presumes that an event produces another event (i.e., A causes B).

Channel The medium through which a message is communicated.

Chronological pattern One of four organizational patterns for the body of the speech using a time sequence.

Claims Arguments or positions founded in research-based materials.

Clarity A criterion that requires a speech to be delivered in readily or easily understandable language.

Colloquium A small-group speech format in which a panel of experts is asked questions by a listening audience.

Communication apprehension A natural, controllable fear of public speaking.

Comprehensive A criterion that research should be thorough and complete.

Concept An abstract ideal, value, or belief.

Concise/Conciseness A criterion in which the speaker uses only enough words to convey the fullness of an idea.

Concrete Tangible.

Conclusion A speech summary; includes no new argument or information.

Constructive evaluation Positive feedback comparing a speech to standards of rhetorical practice.

Credible/Credibility A criterion that research be from a believable source.

Current A criterion that research must be new enough to support the claims in the speech.

Deduction A reasoning pattern in which reasoning proceeds from the general to a specific.

Definition A type of evidence that describes a term used in the speech.

Delivery A canon of rhetoric that deals with the speaker's presentation skills.

Discrete The quality of an outline in which each idea is separate and distinct.

Diversity The condition of being different in factors such as gender, ethnicity, and culture.

Documentation Citation of the source of evidence.

Evaluative feedback Responses that signal the speaker as to how the speech was received by the listener.

Evidence cards A means of recording and using non-original information; usually a 4 × 6 card.

Example Single occurrence of an event; graphic depiction of the abstract.

Extemporaneous Type of speech delivery that is rehearsed but not memorized or read from a manuscript.

Feedback Audience response to the verbal and nonverbal cues of a speaking source.

Forum A small-group public speaking format that invites structured participation by an entire audience.

Generalization Drawing a general conclusion from the analysis of specifics.

Groupthink A phenomenon wherein individuals withhold their minority opinion and either remain silent or verbally agree with the group.

Hearing The physical process of receiving signals, which can be interpreted by listening.

Illustration An extended example.

Imagery Vivid language that brings words to life.

Indictment Harm that exists in a present policy; a charge against society.

Induction A general reasoning pattern that proceeds from the specific to the general.

Inflection Variation or change in vocal pitch.

Informative speaking Communication with a goal of reflecting information and ideas.

Interpersonal Communication with a limited number of other persons; the form of comunication in which we attempt to convey to other people those things we have internalized.

Intrapersonal Communication within ourselves; internal communication; the form of communication denoting communication within ourselves.

Introduction The element of the speech, at the beginning, that gains the attention of the audience and states the thesis.

Invention A canon of rhetoric that encompasses the speaker's character and his or her resources.

Jargon Professional terminology; if unfamiliar to the audience, should be explained.

Justification An argument for the workability of a plan presented in a persuasive speech.

Language A system of signs and signals that give meaning to communication.

Leadership The role of organizing and directing people or groups toward completing some task.

Library databases A large, regularly updated file of online citations, abstracts, and full-text documents.

Listening A process of hearing, attending, understanding, and remembering messages.

Logical pattern An organizational pattern that organizes the body of the speech in a problem–solution format.

Main points Direct support for the thesis.

Manuscript delivery Speaking from a script.

Mass media A form of communication aimed at a large number of people, usually without the benefit of feedback.

Mechanical noise Interference in the channel of communication.

Memorized delivery A speech format that is committed to memory from a manuscript; the presentation relies on memory, without referring to the manuscript.

Message The verbal and nonverbal content of public speaking.

Metaphor Implied comparison between two totally different things that have something in common.

Model legislation A plan that has been implemented successfully and serves as justification for similar plans.

Monotone Vocal quality characterized by a lack of inflection.

Noise Interference with communication.

Open-ended question A question that cannot be answered by a yes or no response.

Oral documentation Citation of the source of evidence used in a speech.

Organizational patterns Strategies for organizing the body of the speech.

Outline A written "skeleton" representation, in proper order and sequence, of the main points and subpoints of what the speech will cover.

Overview A statement that forecasts the major points of analysis in the body of the speech.

Panel discussion A small-group presentation of information or ideas to a listening audience, often followed by questions from the audience.

Pause A purposeful break, or moment of silence, in the delivery of a speech that serves as emphasis or underscoring a point.

Persuasive speaking A form of public speech that attempts to convince listeners that something is factual, that something is valuable, or that some policy should be adopted.

Pitch The perceived highness or lowness of the voice.

Policy analysis Examination of the rules and public legislation that govern our lives.

Primary group The classification of group that provides basic needs vital for survival, such as family, friends, and companions.

Process speech A speech that explains in step-by-step detail how something is done or how something is made.

Progression In an outline, ideas following a natural or logical sequence.

Projection Gearing one's energy, vocal variety, and message outward, toward the audience.

Proposition of policy The thesis sentence for a persuasive speech on a question of policy.

Public speaking Live communication to a large group of people.

Question of policy A question that asks for a general solution or plan of action.

Rate The speed at which a person delivers a public speech; measured in number of words per minute, 90–140 words per minute.

Reasoning The process of drawing conclusions from evidence.

Receiver The person who hears a message from another person and attributes meaning to the message.

Reflective thinking model A framework developed by John Dewey to organize and direct the efforts of small groups in the problem-solving process.

Remembering The final step in the process of listening, in which a message becomes a part of memory.

Research The search to find evidence to support arguments.

Research criteria Information that is current, credible, and comprehensive.

Rhetorical question A question that the speaker asks but does not expect the audience to answer.

Secondary group A classification of group as one that is organized for the purpose of completing a task.

Semantic noise Language differences between speaker and receiver (or audience) that interfere with the message.

Simile An explicit comparison between two different things that have something in common and usually contain the word "like" or "as."

Slang Specialized vocabulary that excludes others.

Small group A limited number of people (3–15) engaged in face-to-face interaction in an effort to achieve an interdependent goal.

Source The initiator of a message.

Spatial pattern An organizational pattern that organizes the body of the speech according to location in place, or geography.

Speaking notes A topical, key-word outline developed from a finished-sentence outline.

Speaking rate The normal pace in a public speech, usually 90–140 words per minute.

Speech/thought differential The difference between speech rate and thinking rate (thinking is more rapid).

Statistics Numerical support for a speech, used to prove significance.

Style A canon of rhetoric concerned with the choice and arrangement of words that express a speaker's thoughts.

Subpoints Direct support for the main points in a speech.

Symposium A small-group speaking format that consists of a series of set speeches by each member.

Testimony Expert opinion.

Thesis A single declarative sentence, near the beginning of a speech, that provides the central idea of the speech.

Topic A general area to be analyzed as a part of the speech process.

Topical pattern An organizational pattern that organizes the body of the speech according to subject matter.

Transition Statements that link major ideas of a speech, usually by forecasting and summarizing.

Understanding Attributing meaning to a verbal or nonverbal message.

Validity Having sufficient evidence to support a conclusion.

Volume The perceived loudness or softness of the voice.

Index

Franklin D. Roosevelt once famously instructed that the key to a good speech was to

"Be Sincere, Be Brief, and Be Seated."

If only it were that simple.

Effective communication is one of the most desired skills we can possess. Regardless of a person's profession, community, or network, the ability to communicate well and purposefully is necessary. An essential component in the communication process is speaking.

This book provides the concepts, ideas, and strategies that promote a positive classroom experience and will enable you to transmit this knowledge and training to the world beyond the classroom. You will have the opportunity to demonstrate what you learn, to create and present public speeches, and in the process teach others about topics and issues.

Features:

- Encourages students' reading and retention through clear, precise writing style
- Addresses communication apprehension and how to meet it head-on
- Grounds public speaking and listening in a citizenship context
- Offers many suggestions for proper outlining, organization, and referencing
- Encourages students to examine diversity issues
- Concludes each chapter with review items for discussion
- Includes a brief and helpful chapter on "giving the first speech"

Throughout your college experience and in your future career you will be expected to speak publicly. Your ability to speak effectively and with conviction will be a measure of your professional success. This book provides you the tools for learning and practicing the crucial lifelong skills of public speaking.

ISBN 161731177-4

90000

9 781617 311772

Public Speaking
Strategic Choices

Seventh Edition

Laurie L. Haleta